ACTING IN CHICAGO
For Kids And Parents

Other books by Chris Agos:

Acting In Chicago, 4th Edition

The Voice Over Startup Guide:
How To Land Your First VO Job

Commercial Voice Over Strategies:
Tell A Story, Land The Job

Visit complete-voiceover.com and
actinginchicago.com to learn more.

ACTING IN CHICAGO

For Kids And Parents

How To Launch And Grow
A Young Performer's Career

CHRIS AGOS

All content copyright © 2023 Chris Agos. All rights reserved. No part of this document may be reproduced or transmitted in any form or by any means (electronic, mechanical, photocopying, recording, or by any information storage and retrieval system or otherwise) without the prior written permission of the publisher.

Limit of Liability and Disclaimer of Warranty: The publisher has used its best efforts in preparing this book, and the information provided herein is provided "as is." The publisher makes no representation or warranties with respect to the accuracy or completeness of the contents of this book and specifically disclaims any implied warranties of merchantability or fitness for any particular purpose and shall in no event be liable for any loss of profit or any other commercial damage, including but not limited to special, incidental, consequential, or other damages.

Trademarks: This book identifies product names and services known to be trademarks, registered trademarks, or service marks of their respective holders. They are used throughout this book in an editorial fashion only. In addition, terms suspected of being trademarks, registered trademarks, or service marks have been appropriately capitalized, although the publisher cannot attest to the accuracy of this information. Use of a term in this book should not be regarded as affecting the validity of any trademark, registered trademark, or service mark. The publisher is not associated with any product or vendor mentioned in this book except where otherwise noted.

Sharing this Document: Countless hours of research were spent to create the contents of this book. The information contained in this book has tremendous value, and you may find yourself wanting to share it with classmates, friends, neighbors, and co-workers. However, the information in this document is copyrighted and cannot be shared without the written consent of the publisher. By purchasing this book, you agree to those terms and to use it for your benefit only. It is the sales of this valuable information that will make updates possible as the world of acting in Chicago changes. If enough people disregard that simple economic fact, updates will not be viable or available.

While every effort was made to ensure the accuracy of the information provided in this document at press time, details are subject to change. All of the editorial content in this document is the sole opinion of the author. No fees or services were rendered in exchange for inclusion in this publication.

ISBN: 979-8-9881753-0-8

Visit www.actinginchicago.com for LCCN information.

For more information contact:

www.actinginchicago.com

About the author

Chris Agos began his acting career in 1995. No one noticed. Eventually that changed. Known for his efficiency and professionalism on the job, over 500 different producers have cast him in over 4000 projects in Chicago and beyond. He is the author of several books for actors, including *Acting In Chicago, 4th Edition, The Voice Over Startup Guide,* and *Commercial Voice Over Strategies.* He continues to audition, work, and help other actors get what they want from their acting careers. A Chicago native, he lives in Los Angeles with his wife and twin sons.

Follow:

- Insta: @ChrisAgos
- Twitter @ChrisAgos
- YouTube: chrisagosactor
- Facebook: ActingInChicago
- IMDb: imdb.me/chrisagos
- Reels And VO demos: www.chrisagos.com
- Downloads And Blog: www.actinginchicago.com

Contents:

Chapter 1 – Information Overload 1
Chapter 2 – Setting Expectations 7
Chapter 3 – A Little Background 13
Chapter 4 – Categories Of Work 25
Chapter 5 – Training In The Midwest 37
Chapter 6 – The Right Tools For The Job 49
Chapter 7 – The Actor's Resume And Online Casting Profiles 61
Chapter 8 – Agents In Chicago 79
Chapter 9 – Auditioning In Chicago 109
Chapter 10 – Self-Taped Auditions 125
Chapter 11 – Callbacks In Chicago 141
Chapter 12 – Work Permits, Minor Trust Accounts,
  And Working Conditions 151
Chapter 13 – Being The Choice 157
Chapter 14 – The Actor's Union 183
Chapter 15 – An Actor's Income 203
Chapter 16 – Advocating For Your Child 241
Chapter 17 – Child Actors And Social Media 251
Chapter 18 – Wrap Up 259

Acknowledgments 263

CHAPTER 1

Information Overload

As the parent of young twin boys, I love it when one of them shows an interest in something productive. Sports, STEAM activities, clubs at school; if it doesn't involve a screen and it gets their attention, my wife and I jump into action! We encourage them to do as much as they can with that activity. We even offer up the idea of additional classes, coaches, or lessons to really stoke their interest. Sometimes this approach goes over well, other times the eye rolls tell us everything we need to know.

A lot of parents do this. We all want our kids to be interested in something, especially in an era when it's easy to be endlessly transfixed by blinking pixels. Part of our job as parents is to encourage kids to try a variety of activities so they can discover what speaks to them.

But there are plenty of things that my wife and I know very little about. When our boys come home talking about one of them, it's good to get some background information before jumping into the "classes, coaches, lessons" routine.

For example, one of our sons has just gotten into 3D printing. It sounds fun (in a science-y kind of way), kind of expensive, and a little complicated. But it also sounds like it could have some future benefits. If he gets really into it, maybe it could open some doors for him into the science and tech world. Because I don't know much about it, I grab my phone and search it up like any modern parent.

Between Google, YouTube, Reddit, blogs, social media, industry publications and podcasts, it feels like there isn't anything we can't learn online. What a time to be alive! But this sometimes presents a new problem. We have to sift through all that random information, find what we're looking for, determine the quality of the source, evaluate what's being presented, determine if the activity is something worth pursuing, and finally, decide if it's something that's right for our kids. Often that means a lot of fruitless time spent in front of a screen. For me, trying to learn about something this way is a lot like shopping at IKEA, where I can never find what I'm looking for because there's too much to look at. I usually give up and go home empty-handed.

This reality is what makes a resource like *Acting In Chicago for Kids and Parents* more valuable than ever. If you have a young performer in the house (or maybe you're a young performer yourself), and they're curious about pursuing the business professionally, you not only need information, you *desperately* need information. The world of professional acting is large, complicated, and can be difficult to navigate. It also tends to be a closed world, with gatekeepers who guard the rules, protocols, and terminology that can be difficult and expensive for newcomers to learn. Those rules? Many of them are unspoken. Parents can spend a lot of valuable time trying to decode everything. My goal is to simplify and demystify all of it to remove any confusion.

Many children grow up exploring acting in school plays,

Information Overload

community performances, and productions at houses of worship. Most don't think about acting much beyond these easy and freely available opportunities. But some kids (and their parents) are different.

Is there a kid in your life who has bigger dreams, ones that go beyond the school play? What if they imagine themselves being in a movie or TV show, or romping around in a fun commercial? There are plenty of kids who perform professionally and earn real dollars doing it. Could yours be one of them? Possibly! But there's a lot to know before you venture down that road.

If your only connection to the world of professional acting is the end-product – the movies, TV shows, musicals and other entertainment we watch all the time – you probably have a lot of questions about how kids actually get to appear in those things. You might wonder if your kid needs an agent. Will they be "discovered"? Do young actors even get these jobs in the Midwest? Is it legal for kids to work at very young ages? Are there laws regarding how parents should handle kids' earnings? These are just a few of the many questions I've been asked by parents over the years, and they're the reason why this book exists.

People come to me for answers because I've made my living as an actor and voice over (VO) artist for over 25 years. I've spent thousands of hours working in front of cameras, microphones, and crowds. If you're curious, you can look me up on IMDb. When you do something enough, eventually you're asked to start teaching, which is what I began doing about a decade into my career. During my first few classes, I was surprised to hear my students all asking the same questions. In 2010, I wrote a book called *Acting in Chicago* to provide answers. It's the predecessor to the book you're reading now, and it quickly became the go-to guide for actors looking to launch or grow a career in the Midwest. I'm humbled that the book is in its 4th edition, still helping actors all these years later. It's used in college classrooms and is recommended by acting schools. Dog-eared, marked-up copies are passed from one actor to another, which is my favorite way it gets around.

A few years later, I wrote a book called *The Voice Over Startup Guide* for aspiring voice over talent. This book is an affordable alternative to taking an introductory level voice over class, since not everyone can invest hundreds of dollars to learn about the business of voice over. I developed a teaching method that combines books, audio files, and sample scripts, which covers most of what a beginning VO class would at a fraction of the cost. I followed that up with *Commercial Voice Over Strategies*, a book that teaches the techniques I use when I do commercial VO jobs. Even after 25 years in the industry, I am still out there auditioning, working, and learning every day.

I'm also the Dad of a young performer. One of my sons is a professional voice actor. He voices characters in animated movies and TV shows, he does commercials, and he even sings a little. His first job was a radio commercial which he landed at the ripe old age of four. So I have been where you and your child are right now, wondering how all of this works.

I want to help make the possibility of acting professionally available to anyone, young or old, who has a passion for it. Once you've entered that world, I want you to know what you're doing so

Information Overload

you and your young performer can be confident as you have a ton of fun. This is important for any actor, no matter their age!

To tackle this task, we'll start with an explanation of the various kinds of work available to child actors in the Midwest. It's common for people to think actors only do TV and movies, but there are many other avenues to explore. We'll then learn about the tools young actors need to get the job done. We'll get into the rules of having a kid in the workforce, and how to get the necessary paperwork together so they can work legally. This step is important, so it can't fall through the cracks.

We'll fully explain the process of auditioning for, and being cast in, each type of work a child might do so parents and kids can know what to expect from a wide variety of circumstances. Because children will be paid for their work, we'll also have a discussion about how much they can earn, and how parents can be good stewards of their kids' finances and stay within the bounds of the law designed to protect young performers.

Along the way, we'll talk about the technology needed to launch a kid's acting career and keep it growing. We'll hear from some parents of kids who are currently working to see how they've navigated this business. And we'll reveal all the unspoken rules and industry terms you're expected to know, but no one will teach you. Every industry has its own lingo, and there's no shortage of it in ours. Normally you would have to discover all these things yourself, but everything will be right here.

There's a steep learning curve in front of those who want to explore acting beyond what is offered in a few classes and summer camps. We're going to bring you up to speed quickly, so you can spend less time figuring out the details and more time helping your child reach their full potential.

Besides having fun, the most important rule actors of any age should remember is that our job is to control what we can control and not worry about all the other things. The parent of the professional child actor also shares this job. You've taken the first step, because one of our very first responsibilities is to ourselves and our education. We are all short on time, and parents know that feeling better than anyone. I hope this book will be a very good use of your time.

And you know what? If after reading this book you wind up thinking, "I don't think this acting thing is for us," that's a win, too. It's much better to find out sooner than later.

Should you decide that acting is right for your family, I'm excited for you. Let's get busy.

CHAPTER 2

Setting Expectations

The Midwest has a booming entertainment industry. It's smaller and more tight-knit than those on the coasts, which is good for players who are looking to gain access to it. Unfortunately its small size doesn't make it any easier to navigate. There's still quite a lot for parents to know, and those who are new to the industry usually have questions, concerns, reservations, and things that just make them go, "Hmm."

When you've got a kid interested in acting professionally, sometimes you wonder about their age. Is there a "good" time to get kids started? I can only tell you that there is no easy answer to this question. Kids vary, job requirements vary, and between those two things there's just no age that is "right" for everyone.

As I mentioned, our son got his start when he was four. But let me reassure you that if your child is older than that and is just getting started, it is not too late for them! I'm always amazed at young actors and their parents who worry that they might be too old to begin. There is no such thing! No one expects kids to have a long list of credits by any particular age, so if you are concerned that you should have started earlier, please don't be. Even if your kid is graduating from high school, it's not too late to make a go of this (but maybe consider picking up a copy of *Acting In Chicago, 4th Edition* since your high-schooler is closer to being an adult than a child).

When a kid is a professional actor, they do a lot of learning. Being an actor is all about listening, following directions, and collaboration. Actors have to think on their feet while staying within the bounds of a pre-determined set of circumstances. These are skills that can translate into any sport, activity, or career kids might have later in life. But the added benefit for Mom and Dad is that child actors earn money for college. Or braces. Or a first car. Have you seen how much these things cost? There's nothing wrong with a kid with an extracurricular activity that helps with future expenses.

When a kid does an acting job, they are paid the same as their adult colleagues. Young performers can make as much as anyone else in this business. We'll get very specific about amounts in a later chapter.

But in order for kids to land those jobs, they first have to know a little bit about, well, acting. Here's some news: I don't think you can learn to act from a book. This goes for kids and adults. You can get an idea of it, but I think developing a good skillset requires training in front of, and getting feedback from, a knowledgable teacher. If you're looking for a book that will turn your young performer into their generation's greatest actor, this isn't it. If you're looking for all the information you'll need to make your child's time in this business as enjoyable and productive as possible, you've come to the right place.

You might wonder why I'm leading off with what this book

Setting Expectations

won't do for you and your kid. It's all about setting expectations. Over the years I've found that keeping expectations in check helps make everything easier. In our house, we underpromise and overdeliver. Our kids know this and understand that it's better to be happily surprised once in a while than to be consistently disappointed. This is a good mental place from which to start when it comes to child actors.

There are no guarantees in this business. You're smart, so I'm sure you already know this. But it's tempting to get drawn into the possibilities this business holds, and I'm not going to lie, there are many. Your kid can wind up being cast in a project that eventually brings about social media stardom, pop song releases, Disney movies and YouTube channels with millions of subscribers.

I like to keep my eye on the big prizes, but I also play games according to the probabilities. I think more about what's probable than I do about what's possible. Those kids whose names you know? The ones with the movies, shows, songs and social stardom? They represent what's possible, not what's probable. Good for them for giving the public what they want while they want it, but they are not the norm.

During your time in this industry, you might come across people who will make big promises about your child's success. These are usually accompanied by a sales pitch, the implication being that if you buy this "training package" or enroll them in that "performance program," they'll be stars in no time. Please walk away from people like that. Run, if you are able. I am all about classes for kids, but some people are better at lining their pockets while boosting the hopes of kids and parents than they are at training kids to be actors.

I get it, "Shoot for the moon because even if you miss, you'll wind up among the stars." That looks great stitched onto a pillow but it should not be your guiding philosophy when it comes to an acting career. A better one might be, "I will do everything possible to be ready for any opportunity that comes my way." That's not as catchy, but it will keep you and your young actor grounded. Just remember that anyone who makes big promises about your kid's acting career is likely trying to extract money from you.

You'll get no such promises from me. But here's what you will get. If you ask my colleagues, you'll find that a lot of people like the way I work because I'm quick and I don't mess around on the set. When I'm working, I'm there for one purpose only: to get the job done. I feel the same way about this book. I'm going to give you all the information I wished my son and I had when we started, so you'll have as much insight as possible into the Midwest's child acting community. I'm going to present that information as efficiently as I can, because there's a lot to know. And most importantly, I'll make sure you'll have what you need to put your young performer on a path that works for them, and for you. Having a professional performer in the family is indeed a family endeavor.

Finally, this book is written from my perspective, which is based on my experience over many years of working combined with the time we've spent guiding our son through the business. We all draw conclusions based on the path we take. Because every young actor's journey is different, these conclusions will vary from actor to actor. The best way to read this book is with an open mind. If something strikes you as contradictory to what you've heard or been told, it

Setting Expectations

doesn't necessarily mean that either view is wrong. It just means that the two perspectives don't align.

It would be impossible to speak to everyone's specific set of circumstances or answer every question out there, but I can promise these things: I promise to spill my guts about everything the business has to offer kids and their parents. I'll even name names. I promise that everything you'll read is true, valid and as current as possible. I promise to be straight with you, even if it's difficult to hear. The world you and your kid are looking to explore is filled with challenges, and if I didn't tell you about its difficult parts, would you trust me to tell the truth about the other parts?

Making all of this information work is up to you and your child. But if our family can do it, yours can, too.

Chapter 3

A Little Background

I'm a big believer in understanding the "why" behind something before investigating the "how". This is especially worth exploring when it comes to child actors.

Usually we see kids getting into this business under two different circumstances: Either an adult makes the decision for the child, or the kid asks to do it enough that the adult eventually agrees. Both are valid. In our case my wife and I made the decision for our son since he wasn't old enough to do it himself, but the best case scenario happens when a kid who's excited about working is paired with a supportive adult who understands the commitment. With this setup, magic can happen.

Young actor Cameron Hoppe has always been unafraid of cameras. When she was 15 months old, Cameron's mom, Allison, scheduled a family photo session. There, the photographer pointed out that Cameron had some qualities she didn't often see in other kids. Cameron was playful and willing to follow simple directions, and when she smiled, her face lit up. It was obvious she was having fun. The photographer suggested to Allison that her young daughter could do some modeling. A few phone calls later, Cameron was

AIC FOR KIDS AND PARENTS — Chris Agos

signed with a talent agency. It wasn't long before she was cast in a commercial for a national brand of diapers.

On the set, Allison could see what the photographer was talking about. Her daughter really did seem to have fun in front of the cameras. She was unfazed by the environment of a film set. While some kids find the lights and other production gear a little scary, Cameron seemed to enjoy all of it, and never got tired of playing with the adults making the commercial. Between all of this and the positive feedback she got from the production team, Allison was convinced of Cameron's potential. As a mom who works full time, she realized her work schedule would sometimes conflict with Cameron's, but she decided that any differences could be worked out.

Today Cameron has many jobs under her belt and is poised to do even more as she gets older. But Allison shared some sage advice. "Your kid has to want it more than you do," she says. A child's acting career works best when it's a partnership between kids and their caretakers. This leads to happy parents and kids, and this is true at any age, from infants to teens.

The Industry's Expectations

Acting is supposed to be fun, but there's a common misconception among parents that acting is just like any other childhood activity like sports, music lessons, or scouting. These things bring a lot of value to kids in the sense that skills are developed as fun is had along the way, but they're mostly recreational. While they are a time commitment, a kid's presence or lack thereof doesn't really impact the

A Little Background

lives of anyone else involved. If a player on the basketball team is absent, the game still goes on.

This isn't true in the world of a professional child actor. This world is a workplace, where kids are given as much responsibility as the adults who work with them. Agents, casting professionals, producers, directors and crews are all working when they interact with kids, and because of that, the stakes and expectations are much higher than they are in the school play.

When a kid is on set, they're at work. Just like any other workplace, a professional set has minimum standards for employees. Among those is that kids and their parents will be on time, be prepared, and do the job to the best of their ability. And in fact, if a kid is a no-show, the job often gets canceled, leaving everyone else with a loss. That loss could impact adults with real bills to pay. Meanwhile, the varsity basketball coach still gets a paycheck if their star shooter misses a game.

"Some parents consider professional acting as a way to get their kids to come out of their shell," says Alexandra Anaya Green, the matriarch of an entire family of actors in Chicago. "That goal could equally be achieved by picking up a new sport without the added industry expectations. Acting as a profession holds higher demands, even for kids, as there are a multitude of businesses and livelihoods at stake."

Higher stakes come with higher rewards. With young professional actors, there's immediate, as opposed to future, money involved. Sometimes quite a lot of it. Sure, a kid can be a talented quarterback for his age, but no NFL team is going to put a child on their roster. In ice skating, there's actually a movement to raise the age of skaters who can compete internationally. There is no such limitation placed on young performers. The kids in Netflix's *Stranger Things*, who were all in middle school when they landed their roles, made around $30,000 per episode in the first season of that show. That's $240,000 for a few months of work.

Does that mean your child will earn that much every time they're chosen for a project? No, those kids are outliers. But it doesn't matter if an actor is earning $240 or ten times that amount, expectations are much higher when acting goes from being an after-school activity to being a job.

Probabilities vs Possibilities

Since we just mentioned a big time TV show, we may as well talk about the "F-word". You almost can't talk about child actors without covering the concept of fame. Parents wonder if their kid could achieve some level of name recognition from their time in this business. Can they? Yes. Will they? That's impossible to know!

Visibility is the thing that makes people famous. When audiences see an actor over and over again, they begin to get more interested in them. For any actor to become famous, they need to be in a project that's has lots of eyeballs on it. Let's look at what shoots in Chicago.

Up until about 2010, there were very few TV shows made locally. That began to change when megaproducer Dick Wolf decided to bring his new show about firefighters to Chicago. No one knew that *Chicago Fire* would air for over a decade, and of course we had no idea it would launch multiple spinoffs. But it

A Little Background

put Chicago on the map of places where TV can get made, and the market hasn't looked back since. As of this writing, there are as many as ten shows currently based in the Midwest. By the time you read this there may be more or less, but as the region's production infrastructure grows, more projects will likely come our way.

All those shows need young performers. You'd think that if the show is going to be made in Chicago that they'd use a lot of local actors, and you'd be right! But there's also a pretty noticeable casting quirk in place. Many projects will bring in their main cast from other markets and leave the smaller roles to local actors. Those smaller roles occupy a relatively small amount of screen time, and once an actor appears in one episode of a show, they aren't able to appear again unless their role is brought back by the show's writers. The main cast, which often comes from a pool of actors that are based in LA, NYC, or even other parts of the world, are given most of the screen time and appear in every episode. These roles are called series regulars. Can a Chicago-based actor land a series regular role? Yes! Is it probable? No. It's possible.

Do movies shoot in Chicago? Yes, but they generally follow the same casting quirks. That's not to say that a Chicago-based kid won't be cast as a main character, it's just more likely they'll play a smaller supporting role.

I think it's important for actors of all ages to imagine themselves going as far as the business can take them, and Chicago has lots of work available for actors up and down the spectrum of experience. But I'd rather see an actor aim for working more consistently than see them trying to become famous. Look at it this way: If you're having fun in the business, you just want the chance to have more of it, and if fame comes your way, that's the icing on the cake.

There's a lot more work available than just TV and film, it's just much less visible. We'll talk more about these other categories of work in a later chapter.

Benefits Of Working In Chicago

If you are new to the business and you're looking to get your kid started, the Midwest is a great place to do so. Here, an actor can learn most everything they need to know about acting for a crowd or a camera and when they're ready, they can take that knowledge elsewhere. After all, Chicago is the third largest market in the country. Some would argue that Atlanta is actually third, given that they do more film and TV than we do. But in terms of sheer size and population density, Chicago comes in behind New York and Los Angeles, which means there's more opportunity for a wider variety of work.

Actually, some would call Chicago the largest theater town in the country. New Yorkers would argue that point of course, but with over 150 theater companies here, there's an awful lot of acting going on. The Midwest is also home to some of the nation's busiest advertising agencies and has a huge corporate video production presence. And Chicago is the casting hub for smaller cities like Milwaukee and St Louis. The bottom line is if your child wants to be involved here, there's no reason why they can't be. Your toughest decision might be where to focus your energy.

A Little Background

Commercial Vs. Theater Actors

When it comes to actors in Chicago, in general, there are two types: the commercial actor and the theater actor. This distinction is important to understand for both adult and younger actors. The basics of the two are the same; both are expected to give a truthful and believable performance. But there are some differences to know.

Generally, commercial actors work in front of cameras and microphones, and their performance is recorded to be played back at a later date. Theater actors work in front of live audiences and their performances are not recorded. What you see is what you get, and the next time it'll be a little (or maybe a lot) different than what you saw the last time.

Different unions watch over each type of actor. The commercial actor may join the broadcast union, SAG-AFTRA. The stage actor might join Actor's Equity Association (AEA). It's possible to join both, of course, but each union has its own specific set of rules regarding when and how you can join. Some actors decide to work without being a member of either union. We'll talk more about them later.

The lifestyle of the two kinds of actors can be very different. Commercial actors work and audition during regular business hours: Monday through Friday, from 9:00 to 5:00. Occasionally they run across a job that shoots overnight, but for the most part acting is, in fact, a day job. For kids and their parents, this presents the challenge of fitting the demands of the business in between the demands of work and school.

In contrast, theater actors work mostly after dark. The larger companies rehearse their actors during the daytime, but performances are almost always in the evenings and on weekend afternoons. The one exception to this is children's theater, which is usually performed during the day. Ironically, these productions don't have kids in their cast for the very reason we just mentioned. Most kids are in school at that time.

If a child actor wants to pursue theater, they'll generally be expected to be available after school and on weekends for rehearsals and performances. A young performer who wants to work commercially will mostly do their auditions in the evenings at home, but will be expected do the job during the day if they're cast.

Luckily, managing auditions and jobs is easier for parents than it ever has been. In the past, every audition happened in a casting office, a theater, or an agent's facility. Some are still done this way, but most have transitioned to a self-taping format. This means that the actor is responsible for doing their audition at home, making it easy for parents and kids to tape after school. When the client insists that an audition be held in person, an effort is usually made to schedule kids after 3:00 PM to minimize the amount of school they'll miss. We'll talk a lot more about self-taped auditions later.

The biggest lifestyle difference between the theater and commercial actor is earning potential. I know I'm going to break a lot of hearts by saying this, but as fun as live theater it is, it doesn't pay very well. There's a small group of Chicago-based actors who work at a very high level and are able to book show after show in venues locally and around the country. These actors can do well financially, but for actors who aren't in this group, the earning potential is much greater in commercial work.

A Little Background

Kids who work in musical theater can stay pretty busy. There are a handful of local companies that produce only Broadway-style musicals. In order to work in musicals, though, it helps to be a strong singer and dancer, as well as a strong actor. Performers who are good in all three disciplines are rare, so they tend to work a lot. And in Chicago, there is always a musical being produced somewhere. So if your child is the musical type, they could go from job to job and they'll have some nice earning power as they do something they love.

Is there cross-over between the two worlds? Sure. Actors move between live and taped performances all the time, despite the scheduling challenges. But the greatest volume of work is likely to be in the commercial world, since there is only so much theater being produced at any one time.

You won't need any help from me to participate in theatrical productions. Theater is a very open world, especially for kids. Between local performing arts schools, dance groups, youth groups and community theaters, there is no shortage of opportunities for kids to get on stage. Many non-equity theater companies post auditions online and these notices blast through local acting communities pretty quickly. If your child isn't active in a performing arts group, you can do a little googling and snag an audition for them on your own.

That's very different from the commercial side of the business. This world is much more closed off from public view, and getting these auditions typically requires a relationship with a talent agent. Producers of these projects don't post audition notices publicly, and they don't let just anyone audition.

This is the fundamental reason why *Acting In Chicago for Kids and Parents* exists. Because the commercial world is more closed off, reliable information is harder to come by. So from this point forward, we're going to focus on that end of things.

What's A Workday Like?

If you read this far and are freaking out just a little bit about how this business operates during school hours, take a deep breath. Most kids don't have a lot of industry-related demands placed on them during the day, at least not all the time. Plus, if things get to be too hectic you can always pass on an opportunity. There's no rule that says you have to do everything that comes along.

A Chicago actor's day can be filled with auditions and jobs, or it can be filled with nothing more than scrolling through the social platform of the moment to see what everyone else is doing. Let's take a look at a day with a little bit of everything going on.

A ten-year-old actor, we'll call her Faith, starts her day by getting ready for school. She does her morning routine, packs up her backpack and heads off for a typical day in the 5th grade. She's in the school musical, and she's supposed to be off book (have everything memorized) by this week, so on the way to school she quizzes herself on her lines. After school she and her mom head right to her first audition of the day, a callback for a commercial that shoots next week. A callback is a second-round audition, meaning the producers have seen an actor once, but they want to see them again.

The callback is at a casting director's office, which happens much less these days than it used to. It's for an automaker, and

A Little Background

they're looking to cast a friendly-looking family to be featured shopping for, and buying, one of their cars. After she's paired up with her actor mom and dad, the whole "family" goes into the audition room, where the camera broadcasts her audition to multiple locations around the country: the client in Philly, the agency in Detroit, a producer in Denver, and the director in Los Angeles. A session runner from the casting office is the only person physically in the room with the hastily-assembled family of shoppers.

When she gets home, she helps her mom put together her self-tape setup (more on this later) because her agent sent her an audition for a corporate video project. A fast food chain is looking for someone to play a kid interacting with their new screen-based ordering system inside their restaurants. The audition isn't due for another couple of days, but she likes getting things out of the way early. After she and her mom do a couple of takes, her mom works on editing the file and Faith settles into doing some homework. When the audition is uploaded to the agent, it's time for dinner. After that, Faith has free time until it's lights out.

If you're a parent and you're thinking that this little girl seems pretty self-sufficient for her age, you're right. Her Mom or Dad would probably be keeping her on schedule, returning emails from agents, handling scheduling and submitting files and auditions. All parents are accountants, consultants, cheerleaders, drivers, and administrative assistants to their kids. When you're the parent of a child actor you can add director, lighting technician, editor, director of photography, audio engineer, hair and wardrobe stylist and personal shopper to that list. But hey, it's all for a good cause.

This imaginary day had a lot of good things going on. Faith laid the groundwork for future work, and that's one of the main aspects of the job. Actors can have many days just like this, but they can also have nothing to do at all. Sometimes you're up, and sometimes you're not, and that's the nature of the business.

But before you think about agents, self-taping and callbacks, it's good to know more about the different types of work that are available to young performers. This will help you decide where you might put your energy, so let's talk about that next.

CHAPTER 4

Categories of Work

Every family is different. Some have lots of time and resources to invest into a child's career, others have to jump through hoops to support their child's acting. No matter which kind you belong to, there should be some benefit for all the time and effort you and your kid will put toward the industry. Sure, we want our kids to grow and be creative and have fun, but if you're going to invest significant family time and resources, it should amount to more than a good time. It should at least cover the costs that come with being in this business.

We're going to focus on the parts of the business that pay well. I believe it's worth exploring these things and possibly even focusing on them since regular cash flow helps grease the wheels of any career path.

There are several ways (besides theater) that Chicago's young performers can use their acting skills and be paid handsomely for them. I'll explain each one. You know what some of them are but the meaning of others may not be so obvious.

AIC FOR KIDS AND PARENTS — Chris Agos

Commercials

Commercials (also called spots) are exactly what you think they are. They advertise products and services on TV, in movie theaters and online. They range from :05-second YouTube pre-rolls to :120-second ads for pharmaceuticals. They can be annoying, intrusive and loud, but they make good money for the actors who appear in them. Some performers make the bulk of their income from commercials.

I think it's important to understand how a spot gets made so you can understand where the actor fits into the process, so let's take a simplified look at the life of a spot from start to finish.

A commercial starts with a product or service that needs some publicity. Let's say it's a new car. The car is made by a company, which hires an advertising agency to market the car. The ad agency people talk with the car company people about how they think the car should be promoted, what kind of image it should have, who the target buyer might be, and other things that will shape how the car will be marketed. Then the ad agency people come up with a few ideas for the car company to look at.

During this process, someone comes up with a concept for a commercial. Multiple concepts are considered by the creative team, the people who are in charge of executing the company's marketing vision. When a concept is agreed upon, commercial scripts are written and submitted for approval. Let's say one of those gets green lit for production. The ad agency then hires a production company, which is a firm that specializes in the production of commercials, hence the name. The production company works with the ad agency to make sure the spot comes out exactly as it was pitched to and approved by the car company. So they hire the crew (a director, set designers, wardrobe stylists, etc.) and they hire the actors. The production company holds an audition, often run by a casting director. A casting director's job is to sort through all the talent (meaning actors) that might be right for the spot, bring them in to audition, and present the results to the production company and the ad agency, who will ultimately decide (sometimes with the input of the client) which actors to use. Once the actors are chosen, the spot gets made, aired, and then retired when it's no longer needed.

We'll talk more about casting directors and auditions later. But I wanted to give you an idea of how complex the process is before actors ever get involved. Commercials are open to all ages and types of actors: young, old, beefy, skinny, quirky, intellectual, goofy, and everything in between. Kids who are super personable typically do well in commercials, since you can't really hide your personality from the camera.

Industrials

The word "industrial" is a loose term, but generally refers to productions not seen by as wide of an audience as a commercial. They are produced for a specific group of people. Sometimes this group includes members of the general public, other times just the employees of a company. Industrials are paid for by corporate entities instead of creative ones, yet they don't always pitch products. Often they're used to inform instead of promote.

Let's say a company wants to get some product information into the hands of American farmers. They can do it effectively by producing a video that's just shown to farmers, either by streaming it on a targeted website or by mailing the farmers a DVD (yes, people still watch DVDs, especially in the Midwest). This allows the company to bypass the expense and time constraints of a TV spot, and reach their audience much more efficiently.

These videos are maybe five or ten minutes long, and very often they need actors. Sometimes actors are hired to play out a scene (like two farmers talking about the product) and sometimes an actor is hired to portray a member of the company, like a spokesperson. If the actor talks directly to the audience by looking into the camera, that's called on camera narration. Kids can be hired for both types of roles.

Another example of an industrial is a training video. Let's say that a car manufacturer wants to inform its dealers about the updated safety features in their cars. To do this, they decide to produce a video with all the details. Instead of just showing the features and telling the dealers about them, they cast a family of four. The audience sees them them using the car in their daily life. They run errands, drop off and pick up kids at school, and engage with the car's systems the whole time. Scripts are carefully written to show the car doing its thing, and the scenes will show the family interacting with it in specific ways. The idea is to put together a video that helps dealers remember the safety systems, and thus be able to use them in their sales pitches with potential customers.

Chicago is a big market for this kind of work. This is the one thing we do more of than any other market in the country. Some people build whole careers around industrial work. It's pretty rare for kids to be used as the narrator of an industrial, but it happens!

Categories of Work

Most often, kids are shown playing out a scene like the ones described above. These are high paying jobs, so even though they may not sound all that interesting, this is a corner of the market that should not be ignored.

Voice Over

When you watch a show or commercial on TV and a voice is heard but not seen, you're listening to a voice over (VO). People who do voice over work are called voice overs, voice actors, or voice talent. Any way you say it, there are lots of opportunities for kids in this part of the business.

Voice talent work in all kinds of media: TV, radio, film, commercials, industrials, web, video games, toys, audiobooks, children's books, and elevators (you know, the lady who says "25th floor" when you get out on the 25th floor?) I was even the voice of a treadmill – no, I'm not kidding. There's a company that used to make a machine with virtual personal trainer feature. It was supposed to help motivate you through your workouts and you could pick between a male or female trainer. I was the voice of the guy.

My son works almost exclusively in voice over. Back when he was a preschooler, I would literally hold his hand through the entire process. Today, he's much older and wiser (don't tell him I said that), and he handles most auditions on his own. When he books a job, he does 99% of it by himself. The only thing I do is make sure the paperwork is filled out correctly. While he started in commercials, he mostly works in animation now.

Whenever I teach VO, there's usually someone in class who

29

thinks doing voice over is all about the quality of your voice. They think that if you have the voice for it (whatever that means to them), you'll get work. This may have been true in the past, but the quality of your voice is much less relevant than it used to be. If you think of your voice as an instrument, what counts today is how you play it. Being a good voice talent is more about the read, or how the script is delivered, than how your voice literally sounds.

This is true with kids, but what is front and center for young voice talent is how old they sound. Producers usually have roles that call for a specific age range. Because kids grow and change so quickly, young voice talent can pass through several age groups during their career. When my son got his first job, he sounded like a preschooler but he would also get auditions that called for toddlers or even babies! As he aged, we found there was a lot of demand for voices in the 8-11 age range. He's currently in middle school and has that awkward vocal quality where he doesn't quite sound like a kid anymore, but you also wouldn't mistake him for an adult.

But again, it's not just about how kids sound. Most voice talent are judged by what they can do with the script. The challenge for producers is to find performers who sound young and also have the ability to take direction and make adjustments during the recording session. They sometimes solve this problem by hiring older kids who can sound younger, like a twelve-year-old whose voice hasn't started changing. This is sort of the sweet spot for a lot of kids. Their young voices are perfect for a project, and their experience and maturity makes them easy to work with.

I'll go over some of what's involved in working in VO, but for a deeper dive check out my book *The Voice Over Startup Guide:*

Categories of Work

How To Land Your First VO Job. This part of the business has some hoops to jump through, and you can't just wing it. A home recording setup is a must for all of today's voice talent because we're expected to do our auditions and work from home. You don't have to break the bank, but there are some items that are worth investing in. Putting together your first setup can be daunting, so in addition to writing *The Voice Over Startup Guide*, I've put together a free VO resource guide to make the process simpler. Download it from actinginchicago.com.

A word of caution: Talent with speech issues such as a lisp or a stutter should work with a therapist to mask as much of it as possible before pursuing this kind of work. If a job requires a kid with a stutter, a producer will likely hire a talent they know and tell them to do the stutter rather than look for someone who actually has one.

The bottom line is VO can be a lucrative addition to your child's actor tool box. Later I'll talk about how much voice actors can make.

Commercial Print

The term "print" covers any job where an actor's photograph is taken with a still camera. The term "commercial" means the image is used to promote something. The photo might be used anywhere, such as online ads, trade publications, product packaging, mailers, point-of-purchase displays, billboards or catalogs. Agencies generally want to cast kids who look like normal, everyday kids who you might see at any playground or school.

For obvious reasons, this work is all about how you look. If your young performer has the look the client is hunting for, they'll be in the running for the job. The acting thing is secondary, though it still counts because all print jobs are going after some kind of "feel" the model must emote. The client might need someone to be really excited, confident or confused, and the actor they hire has got to be able to connect with that state of mind and actually look excited, confident or confused.

Sometimes print jobs come as a bonus with on camera jobs like commercials and industrials. I once did a series of TV spots for a medical association, and they also wanted to use my image in their print campaign. The print work was negotiated as a separate job with its own fee, because the TV shoot only entitled them to use my likeness for TV. So for that job I was paid twice: once for broadcast use and once for print.

A lot of kids will do catalog work. This term is a holdover from the old days, but the concept is the same. A kid, or a group of them, will be hired to play with a toy, or pretend like they're on a family camping trip, or doing some other activity. Photos from these shoots are usually used to generate sales online.

Occasionally producers will look for kids with specific skills or experience. For example, a music school might put out a call for kids who play certain instruments in the hopes that casting these kids will bring some authenticity to the photo shoot. In cases like these, the kid who books the job not only has the look the client is going for, but familiarity with something specific that will make the job easier for everyone.

Print is great work because the jobs are usually quick and pay fairly well. The downside is that it takes longer to get paid for print

Categories of Work

work for a variety of reasons, one of which is that it's not covered by a union. More about unions later.

TV/Film

Of all the jobs available to Chicago actors, these are the ones everyone wants. Unfortunately they're also the toughest to book. It's common to see Chicago actors with ton of credits for other forms of work, but no TV or film roles

The issue isn't the lack of available opportunities. The challenge is that not every project has kids written into the script, and when they are, a call is put out for specific ages and types. Only actors who match the role's age and type requirements are asked to audition. Plus, the number of actual audition spots is limited to just a few. This means not every kid is going to be able to audition for every role that's available, even the ones for which they're right.

But when they have young roles to fill, TV shows like to cast local actors. Not only can local kids get the job done, but they cost producers less than bringing someone in from out of town.

Most of the main actors in a show will come from other markets like LA or New York. Those actors are going to be here a while, so they're put up in hotels or apartments, and sometimes given things like per diem payments and car allowances. Also, minors are always accompanied by an adult, meaning producers have to pay for a second person's expenses, too. So it's most likely that Midwestern kids will work on the projects that shoot here.

Film work is difficult to get in Chicago because there's so little of it. I should make a distinction here: Hollywood-based film work is scarce, but there are plenty of student and independent films produced all the time. There's room for both in an actor's career, but there's a big difference in how we're hired.

For the big budget studio films, nearly all of the main actors are cast in other markets. That means Chicagoans don't usually have a shot at those roles. We get the smaller parts, which sometimes can be really good ones. To be considered for this work, you have to be called in by whichever casting director is working on the film, which is usually Claire Simon Casting, PR Casting, and Karge+Ross Casting. Another large office, O'Connor Casting, does work on film, but their strength lies in casting for commercials, industrials, and even print and VO jobs. I'll explain more about how casting directors work in a bit.

Independent films with smaller budgets sometimes use casting directors, but they might just call agents directly for auditions. Ultra low budget and student films, on the other hand, usually bypass the traditional casting avenues and find talent in other ways, like posting in Facebook groups. These are a crapshoot in the sense that you never know what the experience will be like, so my advice is to avoid these kinds of projects unless you know the people involved. You and your kids have more productive things to do.

Wrap Up

You can think of the different types of work as bricks in the actor's career wall. An industrial brick is laid next to a VO brick, which is resting on top of a TV brick and all three of these are supported by a commercial brick. Why? Because Chicago is the *third* largest

Categories of Work

market in the country, not *the* largest. There isn't enough of one kind of work here to let everyone focus only on the one thing they really want to do. Actors are much more likely to be working in multiple disciplines, with the rare exception of course. There are some people who do very well focusing on print, and some just work in VO. But for the rest of us, we work on building our wall.

A strong foundation of knowledge is the only way to make sure your child's wall is going to hold up. Most kids need some training, and you're in luck because Chicago is a great place to learn.

CHAPTER 5

Training In The Midwest

There's a lot of thought that goes into where we send our kids for training, no matter the activity. In our house we think about the cost, the convenience factor (how far away from home and school the activity is) and the reputation of the facility and its staff. We also think about what we want our kids to get from the experience. Are we simply introducing them to something or do we suspect they have a built-in gift for the activity?

The task of educating young actors falls to independent acting schools, and there are plenty in Chicago to choose from. They aren't affiliated with a college or university and are typically owned and operated by performers (or former performers) themselves. Some schools combine acting classes in addition to other kinds of performing arts like dance and singing. Others will mostly stick to acting, and those are the ones that will be our focus.

Training By Age Group

Most schools offer classes to kids beginning around six years of age. Before that, kids aren't really ready for instruction on acting. Most

AIC FOR KIDS AND PARENTS — Chris Agos

classes for children this young will not look like what you'd think of as a traditional acting class, with actors holding scripts and performing scenes. Little kids need something less structured.

Teaching philosophies vary, but at this age classes will likely look more like playtime than anything. Teachers will have a goal of exploring kids' creativity by tapping into their imaginations. Through the use of games, songs and improvisation, young actors can learn the art of listening and responding, which is foundational to acting.

Scripts usually aren't introduced at this age. Carole Dibo, owner and director of Actor's Training Center (ATC) in Wilmette, IL., says, "The youngest kids should be developing their love of pretending. It's more about finding the joy than looking at scripts. They'll get plenty of that later."

In the early elementary school years, kids begin telling their own stories. Classes likely lean heavily on improvisation as kids build imaginary worlds and inhabit them. The focus is on fun and learning to create. Students might write a scene or a short play together as a group, teaching them team building skills.

Around the 3rd or 4th grade, kids begin to respond well to the idea of saying words that have been written by someone else, or writing words for each other. Instructors might introduce short scripts for commercials, or do scene work in a fun, engaging environment.

By the middle school years, usually the students that get the most out of acting classes are the ones who want to be there. Carole says, "They've got to be invested at this age. Sometimes when it's the parent's choice to enroll a child, typical middle-school self-consciousness can get in the way of them having a good experience."

Ideally students have expressed an interest in acting and are intrigued by the idea of performing. Since this is a time when they're starting to discover who they are as individuals, these can be important years not only for their social development, but also for their acting.

One thing that Carole suggests is to avoid putting students in acting class with their friends. "When that happens, the existing relationship is brought in," leaving little room for spontaneity because expectations are already in place between kids. Students might be reluctant to try something new or take a risk, simply because their friend might make fun of them for it later. Actors have to be willing to put themselves out there, something that's challenging when they're doing it in front of someone they know in another context.

By high school, classes are all about building a base level skillset. "Acting skills are life skills," says Rachel Patterson, director of Acting Studio Chicago (ASC) in Chicago, IL. "Collaboration, empathy, creativity, listening…these are all basic skills that any actor needs to develop, but they're also qualities that are necessary to thrive in adulthood. The arts aren't the only place where we need to work with colleagues, creatively solve problems, and understand that words and actions have an impact on others. Those are skills that are necessary to navigate almost any situation as adults."

Rachel also points out that it's important for any class at this age to meet students where they are. Kids develop and mature on different timelines. "Some come into class unafraid to share their thoughts and opinions, and some take longer to find their own voice," she says. "The important thing is to help them understand that in acting, there is no one right answer or solution to a problem."

AIC FOR KIDS AND PARENTS — Chris Agos

Students often find their niche in the high school years, which can help both their social and professional development. Acting classes are sometimes a catalyst for this process.

There are three schools in Chicago that I recommend for children's classes: Actor's Training Center, Acting Studio Chicago, and The Green Room Studio.

ATC: Actors Training Center, Wilmette, IL.

ATC offers adult classes, but its real strength lies in their programs for young actors. Most schools aim their programs at kids and teens who want to have fun and learn, but aren't necessarily studying in the hopes of establishing a professional acting career. Not so at ATC.

The kids there have fun while they're getting great instruction, but ATC uses a work-based approach to teaching. Classes on everything from acting basics to more advanced topics are designed to challenge and prepare kids for the real world situations in which they'll find themselves if they decide to pursue an acting career.

The school has a national reputation because of relationships it's developed with with casting directors and agents in New York and L.A. These industry insiders periodically come to ATC to run workshops on everything from nailing certain types of auditions to acting while singing, giving kids the chance to work with and be taught by people who cast TV shows, films and Broadway shows.

The youngest kids at ATC work on building imaginary worlds, respecting the choices of others and improvisation. As they age, they'll pick up the basics of story telling and begin learning how to audition for different types of scenarios.

In the high school years, ATC tries to send the message to teen actors that being themselves is enough, there is no need to try and be someone else. This philosophy applies as an acting technique but is also a good for life in general. The school makes a point of encouraging young performers to be their authentic selves instead of put on a show for the world. This can be a tough thing to do for actors of any age!

Check out all of their current course offerings at actorstrainingcenter.org.

Acting Studio Chicago, Chicago IL.

Acting Studio Chicago has been in existence in one form or another since 1981. It was started by actress Jane Brody, who had been working with Michael Shurtleff, a leading casting director and author of *Audition*, an influential book on the audition process (and a great read, I recommend you pick up a copy). Brody realized that his approach to acting was a valuable tool that wasn't being taught in Chicago, so she opened a studio called The Audition Centre to share the method with other actors.

The 1990's brought a change of ownership and a new name. Rachel Patterson, the studio's owner and director for over twenty-five years, has grown it into a well-respected school with a great word-of-mouth following among Chicago's young actors and their parents.

They've accomplished that by striving to give each student a unique experience as they move through their training. Patterson says, "We really pride ourselves on giving personal attention to all our students. We try to be a resource for kids and parents, so even if they're not currently registered in a class, they're always welcome to take advantage of our open door policy. We're happy to give advice on resumes, headshots, or chat about what future steps an actor might take to move ahead in their career."

The pro-level staff at Acting Studio Chicago are more than qualified to guide any young actor through the maze of work available in Chicago. They're straightforward about the realities of the business, but still very supportive of what each actor wants to accomplish.

Parking in their neighborhood is difficult, but they're a short walk from the CTA Red Line. Acting Studio Chicago's youth classes can serve as a one-stop shop to learn all about acting for the camera. Check out actingstudiochicago.com for their current offerings.

The Green Room Studio, Chicago

The Green Room is another stellar place for kids to study commercial acting. Run by Sean Bradley, an actor and former casting associate, it was founded for the purpose of training actors in the art of working in commercials but has since branched into many other things, including classes for kids.

The Green Room's curriculum was drawn from Sean's experience of watching thousands of commercial auditions while working at O'Connor Casting, one of Chicago's busiest casting offices. There he saw the good and the bad, and decided that the city's actors needed to change the way they approach auditioning. Knowing that more producers would cast in Chicago if the talent pool was doing fantastic auditions time after time, The Green Room opened to show good actors how to make their on camera auditions great.

Anne Acker, director of their kids program, agrees that kids thrive when they start exploring their creativity, but adds that the direction should be specific. "We work on practical things like not wiggling in front of the camera, answering questions truthfully but appropriately, and we teach a lot of terminology so the kids know what's being asked of them on set."

One thing unique to The Green Room is that they use games to do a lot of their teaching. One popular exercise is called "The Business Journey," where kids play the casting process like a game. They go through the whole process and play each role in it, while wearing signs that say "agent", "casting", or "client". Anne says, "Kids spend a lot of energy wondering why they didn't get a particular role, and some of that is taken away when we help them understand that the process has less to do with them than it does other things outside of their control."

Visit thegreenroomstudio.tv for their current class schedule.

What To Look For

I've mentioned three schools I'd trust to train my kids, but if they're not a practical option for you, there are some things to look for when choosing a school in your local area.

Start by doing some research on the faculty and staff of the school you're considering. Ideally they'll have some professional experience. Look them up on IMDb (The Internet Movie Database), or on iSpot.tv (a site that catalogues commercials) to see if they've done any broadcast work. If they haven't, they may have experience in theater. That's fine, but harder to verify. You can check to see if they have personal websites or if they're represented by talent agencies. If you strike out on all of these methods, it's unlikely you'll get professional-level instruction at that school. That's not to say that it wouldn't be a fine place to introduce your young performer to acting, but it may not be the place for the long term.

Be cautious of any school, program, or facility that makes promises of any kind. Unfortunately there are companies who see you and your young performer as a revenue source more than anything. If you find yourself feeling upsold, or you're asked to spend thousands of dollars on a package of classes, headshots, and other products and experiences, you might be witnessing a scam. While it's true that you get what you pay for, Rachel Patterson says, "very high costs are a red flag." You shouldn't have to spend more than a few hundred dollars on a class, and there's no need for your child to take more than one at a time.

Be especially wary of places that advertise heavily on social media to get you to contact them or attend one of their conventions. Once you're there, in an effort to separate you from your money they will dangle the success of their "alumni" who have gone on to do amazing things. Do not fall for this. The legitimate decision makers in our industry ignore these companies.

Wherever you land, the most important thing is that the child clicks with the instructors. Being in acting class should be fun and shouldn't feel like work. At the same time, you want the young performer to learn essential skills they can carry with them into later classes.

Training In The Midwest

A Word About Experience

Do the decision makers look for kids who have experience? Sometimes. But you can't get experience without working and no one is born with an impressive resume. Believe me, everyone in the industry understands this conundrum. Starting with a clean slate is accepted and expected, especially when it comes to younger performers.

Most kids who do well in this business aren't very shy. They have none of the hangups that adults might, and they approach each situation as a new opportunity to have fun. But everyone can get nervous, especially when we're thrown into an unfamiliar situation. On set it can feel like you're under a microscope. The intensity of the attention can be nerve-wracking, even for seasoned kids. Experience does increase confidence and that's why it can be important for young actors to spend as much time in front of a camera as possible.

You can help kids by enrolling them in classes, but practicing at home is another option. This is a great use for the camera on your phone. Besides paying for time in a class, I think home practice is the best way for kids to become familiar with the dynamics of working in front of a camera. But I also think this method is most effective when it's done in conjunction with a class. I don't know about your kid, but mine always seems to listen to their teachers better than they listen to me. Sometimes we're saying the same things, but the message carries more weight when it comes from an outside source.

The down side to studying on your own at home is that you've got no one but yourself to tweak your child's performance. Most parents don't have the expertise to give their kid helpful direction

AIC FOR KIDS AND PARENTS — Chris Agos

(at least not at first), so supplement the self-teaching method by allowing your young actor to spend some time with a professional instructor. One thing though: don't post practice clips on social media. Let your kid rehearse without the worry of what their friends and followers will think.

On-Set Learning

You might say, "Well, my kid can just learn on the job." Oh believe me, they'll learn plenty when they're working. In fact, I think work experience beats class experience by a long shot. Directors, other actors, and crew members can provide a wealth of information and helpful tips. But you want them to have at least a little working knowledge before they get cast in a paying job. The key word there is "paying".

Many actors think of the theater as a place to experiment and learn, but it's not a good idea to apply that logic to on camera work. By the time a child is on the set shooting, months (sometimes longer) have gone into planning the job. Concepts were pitched, several versions of the script were written, locations were scouted, props were collected, auditions were held, wardrobe was chosen, and lots of money was spent. Very often the budget is so tight that everything must go according to plan. An eight-hour day just can't stretch into ten, because there's no money left to pay for overtime.

As actors, it's our job to make sure we don't do anything to stretch out the length of the job. That means we're expected to show up on time, know our stuff, and do our job well. Understandably, no one wants to pay an actor to learn on their set, no matter how young and cute they are. They expect kids to be able to do the job. It's a terrible feeling when you see your child looking very uncomfortable doing something they thought they would enjoy. Solve that problem by getting them into a class and practicing at home to stay sharp.

The great thing about taking classes is that kids aren't just going to learn about the subject matter, they're also going to pick up bits and pieces about other aspects of the business. Invariably the discussion will turn to agents, headshots, and other industry-related stuff. Depending on who they hear it from, the information could be spot-on accurate or horribly off track. I'm here to make sure you get the right information. Up next: things every working actor can't live without.

CHAPTER 6

The Right Tools For The Job

You can't play poker without a deck of cards, change a tire without a jack, or play the violin without a bow. Without the right tools, it doesn't matter how much training, experience, or confidence you have, you're simply not getting the job done.

Actors rely on tools, too: A headshot, a resume (paired with an online casting profile), an agent, and a self-tape setup. Without these things, an actor can't do their job. I'll explain what each one is, why they're so important, and how best to use them.

The Idea Behind Headshots

An actor's headshot is the first thing the industry will see when they encounter that actor. The most important thing about a headshot is that it's accurate. It should look like how the performer looks in real life, and should not be over-styled. If you're used to doing pictures for dance recitals or pageants, an acting headshot will be the opposite of those. Natural and clean is the way to go for child actors.

From infancy to around age six, headshots can easily be done by parents with their phones. Take a photo of your child and frame it vertically (like you would for Instagram) and center them in the shot from about their chest to just over the top of their head. Make sure the setting is well lit and avoid any strange shadows in the photo, like what happens when you take a picture of someone standing outside in uneven shade. Also make sure to use a plain background. You don't want anything like signs, other people, or lovely landscapes drawing attention away from the actor. If your phone has a portrait setting, you can use that.

The industry will want to see professional headshots by the time young actors reach first or second grade. This is a bummer for parents since kids grow and change so quickly, and headshot photographers aren't cheap. But the reality is that the business will expect kids to have shots that are comparable to the shots of adult actors.

You might be tempted to use your child's school picture as a headshot. This isn't a good idea. While these pictures are a nice record of what kids look like from year to year, they're not intended to be used in a professional setting. Often the lighting is flat and harsh, and your little one doesn't look their best. We want them to be natural in their headshot, but we also want to have some control over it, which we don't get with school pictures. Give Grandma a copy, but don't distribute them to industry professionals.

Crafting A Professional Headshot

For decades, everyone printed their headshots on paper because we had to hand them out when we went to auditions. Of course, everything's digital now. Instead of deciding on glossy or matte paper, we

The Right Tools For The Job

try to make our headshots look good as a thumbnail online. That's how most decision makers encounter headshots.

Even if you're brand new to this business, you've probably come across an actor's headshot before. They're frequently posted on social platforms. Sometimes they're smiley, sometimes they're super serious, but they're always carefully thought out.

We know that headshots have to be an accurate representation of what the actor looks like in real life. But a headshot should also say something about the actor. We want to give the decision makers an idea of who's looking back at them.

When they're looking at a kid's shot, it's likely that the first thing anyone in the industry is asking themselves is, "What age range can this kid play?" That's because they have a need for a specific age. If they need someone who plays 8-10 and your child looks like they're in that range, they'll give the headshot a closer look. If the headshot makes your child seem younger or older, they'll continue looking for other kids. This is why headshots have to be accurate. If a young performer is given a chance to audition based on an old headshot, but they look a few years older in the audition, you'll have an unhappy decision maker on your hands. Why? Because they need a child who looks 9 and yours looks 12 in real life, meaning that audition spot was taken by someone who isn't appropriate for the role. That's a wasted audition for everyone.

But there's much more to a kid than just their age, so we also have to consider what the shot will convey about the actor. Start by thinking about how the actor shows up in the world. Some kids have a look-at-me vibe, others are more reserved. Some can pull off a snarky attitude, others can do super sweet effortlessly. While we think our kids can do it all, the reality is that the best looks are probably going to be the ones that match their natural personality.

The setting, clothing choice, hairstyle, body language, expression and lighting will all combine to convey a message: this actor's funny, or that kid's super smart. Or that one's cute and cuddly while another leans a little toward the bratty side. We want to craft a truthful shot that draws the viewer in and makes decision makers want to call the actor in.

For this reason, you'll want to work with someone who knows how to pull this off. That person is a professional headshot photographer.

Your Photographer

The photographer will have a great impact on how a performer's headshots will look. Getting a good shot out of an actor is a combination of art and science (especially when it comes to kids), and solid shooters have it figured out.

These folks are easy to find. Start by Googling "Chicago headshot photographers", or scrolling through various actor hashtags on Instagram. There will be tons of sample shots to look at. You'll notice that photographers have different styles. Some shoot with only natural light, others only work in studio spaces with very controlled lighting. Some seem to do a lot of fun comedic shots, others stick with a dramatic look. Not everyone photographs kids, so you may have to ask if you don't see any kids' headshots on their profiles.

A more interesting method of finding a photographer is to visit the websites of agents in town and browse through their talent

The Right Tools For The Job

galleries. When you find a few shots you like, write a short email to one of the agents politely asking which photographer took which shot. Something like this should get a reply: "Hi, I'm the Mom of a young actor and I found a couple headshots on your site that I really like. Would you be able to tell me whom Susan Smith and Daniel Davis used for their shots? I'd appreciate knowing which shooters in town do good work. Thanks in advance for a reply!"

The agent should eventually get back to you. If they don't, either email another one in the agency, or wait a couple of weeks before emailing again. Be persistent without being a hassle. This method does a couple of things: not only does it let you find out who did those shots, but you'll also likely discover who that agent likes to recommend to their talent. If agents are sending their actors to a shooter, it's because the photographer gets good results. And the best part is, you're introducing yourself to an agent, and that could be useful down the road.

The most obvious way to find a good shooter is to ask other actor parents who they've hired. If you're out and about auditioning, working and taking classes, just ask around. You'll probably hear the same names come up.

When you come across someone whose work you like, set up an appointment. Many offer free, no-obligation consultations. It's important to talk with anyone you're considering hiring, either in person or virtually, before you put down any deposits. At this point, you're still doing your research.

During the appointment, you want to look for a couple of things. Some photographers have their own studios. If you meet them there, look around and note the general feel of the place. Do

AIC FOR KIDS AND PARENTS — Chris Agos

you get good vibes? Were you greeted with a pleasant smile when you arrived? Do they make you and your child feel welcome? Is there an air of brisk activity about the place or stifled boredom? Does the studio seem well organized or chaotic? And while you're at it, were you able to find parking? Can you play your own music during the shoot? Also, use the bathroom while you're there, or check out the dressing room if there is one. Are they bright and clean? All of these elements will come together for you and your child on the shoot day, and any of them could affect how you feel, and thus influence the result of your shots.

A lot of photographers don't have studios. Don't be put off by that, there are plenty of good ones who don't have a dedicated space for their business. They shoot at locations around town and do all their post processing at home. At appointments like these, it's less about where you're going to be shooting (although that's definitely a question you should be asking) and more about their policies. Ask about things like deposits, pricing, turnaround times (the time between when the shoot and when you see the proofs), and post processing/editing costs. Some photographers include a certain number of finished images with the price of your session, others charge you for the session and the finished images separately. Most offer different options when it comes to looks.

You can think of a look like a mood change, where you'd use a different background, clothing, and maybe even hairstyle to convey a different idea than one you used before. This is where you would go from, say, a smiley headshot, which is commonly used for commercial auditions, to a more serious headshot, which might be used for TV/Film.

The Right Tools For The Job

While all of these things are good to take stock of, the most important factor in choosing a shooter is how easily your young performer interacts with them. The session should be fun and the photographer should naturally be good with kids. If the opposite is true, it doesn't matter if you've walked into the most well run photography studio in the city, the shots aren't going to come out very well. It's important that kids feel comfortable in front of the camera, which means they have to feel comfortable with the person making their images.

The best photographers are able to not only construct a technically good shot, but also pull out the best looks from their actors. Avoid shooters who might be pushy and believe their way is the only way. You want someone who will work with the ideas you bring into the session.

The Shoot

Once you've found a photographer, it's time to schedule the session. You'll want to think about this a little, because it's not just a matter of when everyone's available. Consider what time of day your actor feels and looks their best. I tend to think more clearly in the morning, but I seem to look better in the afternoon, so I book my sessions after two or three o'clock. My son gets up early like I do, so a morning session would work for him.

When selecting a date, try to make sure that you have nothing else going on that day. This can't always happen, but the idea is to keep the day as stress-free as possible. Try to pick a day when you know things will be predictable and relaxed. And if your kid is dealing with issues like overdue homework assignments or big performances, try not to schedule the session when those can interfere. You want your child's mind to be as quiet and clear as it can be when they're in front of that lens.

Let's say that on the day of the shoot, your actor is able to sleep in a little later than normal. You leave with plenty of time to get to the location. When you arrive, you're able to park easily, you're greeted warmly and feel welcomed by the photographer, and are shown into the clean and well-lit dressing room so you can spread out your stuff. Someone hits "play" on the music you brought, and your kid lights up hearing their favorite song. You spend a little time joking around with your photographer while you choose wardrobe. There's plenty of time to get the session done, your kid is happy and healthy, and they look it. That'll come through in the shots.

In contrast, if you can't find parking and you dash in and people are ticked off that you're late, and they rush you and your child into their crappy dressing room, you're forced to listen to their crappier music, and during the shoot the photographer seems disorganized, that's not going to produce good results. Believe it or not, those negative vibes will come through loud and clear in the photos.

I have made these mistakes. I once hired a photographer based on a recommendation from my agent. I didn't know anything about him other than that he had photographed a lot of actors at my agency, so I booked him based on that.

This guy turned out to be a slow moving train wreck, and it didn't help that I scheduled the session on a day that I had an audition to get to. I arrived at his place on time, and we had four hours to do a two-look session. That should have been plenty of time, but

The Right Tools For The Job

he was not ready for me. His studio was a mess. It was filled with random junk that he had to move out of the way before we could shoot. That took an hour. The whole time he made small talk about nonsense I didn't care about. We didn't look at any of my clothing options until 90 minutes after I got there. We started shooting two hours in. It took him another hour to get the lighting to the point where he was happy with it, and by that time I was done. I wanted to be out of there even though we hadn't yet shot a single frame.

In the end, the headshots were worthless. I tried using them for a few months, but wound up throwing them away because they were so ineffective. They made me look like a stressed-out, unhappy guy, which I'm not! I usually keep one copy of all my headshots for posterity, but I threw those away. That's how little I liked them.

On the other end of the spectrum, there are photographers who will go out of their way to make sure you get the best shots possible. These are the professionals who make the sessions all about the actor, not about the photographer. The good shooters know that it's a team effort, especially when it comes to kids.

Policies and procedures differ but generally things work like this: after the session you'll get thumbnails of the photos. Every usable frame will be posted in an online gallery. There might be hundreds of images to go through. Your task is to narrow them down to just a few favorites. Get comfortable in front of your computer and take a good look at them. Depending on the age of your kid, let them participate in this process. Pick out a few that you think best expresses who the child is, then get outside opinions. If possible, get someone in the business to look at them. Get a teacher, another actor parent, or better yet an agent if you have one, to give you their honest opinion about which shot or shots you could use.

I'm not a fan of posting thumbnails to your socials and letting people chime in. You might get some likes, but most of your followers probably don't know what makes an actor's headshot effective. You want to have someone with a critical eye look at the shots. Your photographer might be one person you could ask for advice since most of them have plenty of experience to back up their opinion.

Once you've selected the winning shots, the shooter will likely do a little post processing on them, cleaning up things like skin blemishes and flyway hairs. Sometimes this service is included in the price, other times it's not, so ask beforehand. Then you'll get the files of your favorites. Often there will be several file types and sizes. You'll have some for printing and posting, and ones that are ideal for certain online casting platforms.

There are differing opinions about whether you still need to have your shots physically printed on 8x10 paper. Physical shots might be down, but I don't think they're completely out. I think there is still a place for prints, so here's my advice: pick your favorite and get a handful duplicated, like 50. It's better to have them and not need them than the other way around.

There are several reputable companies in Chicago that duplicate headshots and any one of them do good work. Look them up on Yelp to get other actors' opinions of them. I work with a duplication house in Los Angeles called Argentum Studios, which I highly recommend. They can do everything online quickly at a reasonable price. You could also ask your shooter who they'd suggest.

By the time you're done hiring a photographer and reproducing

The Right Tools For The Job

the prints, you should expect to spend somewhere between $500 and $700 before the headshots are ready to be seen by the industry. That doesn't include extras like hiring a hair and makeup stylist ($75-$150), paying the photographer a little extra to travel to a shoot location ($100-$250), additional image files ($10-$25 each), retouching your images ($25-$100 each) or buying clothes specifically for the shoot (sky's the limit).

Stick With The Pros

If you're wondering whether it's worth it to spend that kind of money on a headshot, here's your answer: even if this acting thing is just an experiment, you absolutely cannot get away with cutting corners on your young actor's headshot. The biggest issue is credibility. Your child has to look like they belong in the industry with all the other kids who have professional shots. Otherwise, they won't even get in the door.

When an agent is considering a headshot, she'll only look for about three seconds. That's how long the photo has to make the kind of impression it's designed to make. They may look at the resume (more on that in a bit), which sits on the back of a physical photo or comes with a digital one as a pdf. Depending on what they see there, and after determining if they actor could be a good fit for their agency, they'll either save it for later or trash it. And then they'll do the same thing with someone else's shot, perhaps hundreds of times that day. So imagine having a headshot that looks like it was taken by someone's uncle in his back yard. It would eliminate that actor from contention before they even did a single audition. Give your kid the best chance to succeed and hire a real photographer who knows the deal. It'll be well worth the expense.

Below are two Chicago photographers I've worked with. Neither of them paid me for my endorsement. Each has their strengths, and either of them will give you great service at a fair price.

www.brianmcconkeyphotography.com

www.popiostumpf.com

CHAPTER 7

The Actor's Resume and Online Casting Profiles

Now that your young actor has a great headshot, it's time to tell people what they've been up to. Even if the answer to that is absolutely nothing, you'll need a way to give decision makers some idea of who your child is. We do that with resumes.

A resume is a list of stats, credits, and other information that helps decision makers get an idea of how that actor fits into the industry. It's similar to a resume that an adult would put together before a job hunt, but it's a little more personal.

Thanks to the pandemic, we are in this weird transitional time with resumes. Actors can expect to have three versions: a physical resume to be stapled to the back of physical headshots, a digital copy in the form of a pdf, and a one that's part of their profile at certain online casting sites. The rules of resume writing, which we'll get to in a bit, apply to all of them with the exception of formatting. Some of the casting sites will handle that for you. You'll need to format the other resume types yourself, so let's talk about best practices.

The Resume

Resumes are an actor's lifeline to the decision makers. Headshots are the attention getters, but resumes are the substance. So we've got to give them something to look at; something honest, productive and compelling. We also need to organize it in a way that is accepted by the industry.

A resume will always accompany a headshot, even when there's not much work history to list, as is frequently the case with kids. Your child's resume will mostly make the rounds as a digital file, but there are times when physical resumes are requested by a client.

Physical resumes are printed on a piece of paper trimmed to the size of the 8x10 headshot. I take a stack of plain white printer paper to FedEx Office and have them use their flat cutter to trim the whole stack down to 8x10. Then, I print them at home as I need them. I staple a copy to my headshot back to back, so that the viewer can look at the image on one side and flip the shot over to read the resume on the other side. Two staples at the top take care of it. Don't use glue, tape, or more staples than you need. The idea is to make the whole thing look clean and professional.

To create the digital version of your well-crafted physical resume, simply save or export the file from your text editing software as a pdf. This file can be attached to emails and uploaded to casting sites.

As far as those online casting profiles, casting directors in the US and Canada use a handful of websites to organize and send out their auditions. It's imperative that every actor have profiles at these sites. With no profile, there's no chance of being called in, especially

The Actor's Resume and Online Casting Profiles

for film and TV work. You'll have to sign up for at least a basic membership at each one. They are generally free, but some fees do apply. We'll talk more about them in a bit.

The terminology is a little tricky since the casting sites use the word "resume" and "profile" interchangeably. I'll use them the same way, but just know that both refer to the document you put together to show others in the industry what you've been up to.

All the rules that apply to old-school resumes still apply to online profiles, so let's start with the information you should include, how to organize it, and what can be left out.

Building A Resume

Children who are very young don't need resumes. If your child is kindergarten age or younger, the snapshots you take with your phone will be sent to agents and potential employers via email. In the body of the email you'll want to include basic information like the child's name, age and your contact information. If anything else is needed, whoever is doing the asking will let you know.

Resumes come into play once kids have professional headshots. Let's have a look at an example on the following page.

Amy Actor
SAG-AFTRA
amy@amyswebsite.com / Insta: @AmyA

Age: 10 Ht: 4'6"   Wt: 90   Eyes: Brown   Hair: Blonde   Size: Youth S

TV
Kitch Hens	Guest Star	The Eat Network/Donny Director
Bugs Uncovered	Co-Star	ChedderTV/Annie Ant
Space Heroes	Co-Star	NUSA Network/Ernie Spaceport

Film
Selective Hearing	Lead	Movie Studio/Dave Tinitus
The Golden Hammer	Supporting	FilmsPlus/Mallory Mallet

Theatre
Happiness Lives!	Carrie	Lightness Theatre
All For Nothing	Shawna	Roundhouse Players

Industrials
McDowels	Young Customer	McDowels In-House
FireTires	Student	Automotive Voice Productions
Smartdevice	Band Member	RDS Productions

Voice Over

Spots: School Supply, Cute Dolls, OurGym
Narration: Travel Adventures, BounceHuts, Gelson's

Commercial VO - Conflicts available upon request

Education/Training
Acting Level One, Two – Actor School
Improv For Actors, - Improv Studio
Currently in 5th Grade, Washington School, Washtown, IL.

Special Skills/Of Note
Karate (purple belt), french horn, gymnastics, Star Wars megafan, knuckle cracking.

The Actor's Resume and Online Casting Profiles

Feel free to use this one as a guide. In fact, I've created a blank resume template so you can lay out your young actor's resume to match this one. You can download it for free at actinginchicago.com.

This is the resume of a young actor who has had some training and done some work. When an actor is just launching their career, their resume won't look like this. But it gives us something to learn from and, if you're just starting out, something to aim for in the future.

The first thing you'll notice is that the information is logically laid out and easy to read. When an agent or potential employer is looking at a resume, they're likely just glancing at it. That's why we format resumes in the way you see here, since it allows the reader to understand the information quickly.

At the top of the resume you can see the actor's name, union affiliation (more on unions later), and contact information. If the young performer is not a member of a union, you can leave this blank. Don't write "non-union" or "pre-union." However, if the child's union status is Taft-Hartley, include that here. If you don't know what that is, I'll explain it in a later chapter.

I'm not a huge fan of putting personal phone numbers or home addresses on resumes, so list an email address instead. If your child has a social media handle or website that is mostly devoted to their acting work, you can share it here. It's best to only include these if the accounts are being used to promote their work efforts. Definitely be honest with yourself about this and leave it off if it's not work-related.

This would also be where you'd put a link to the child's acting reel if they have one. A reel is a collection of clips from work that the child has done. If you're not familiar with them, have a look at mine by visiting www.chrisagos.com. You can also look up some actor reels when you're browsing the websites of talent agencies. A reel isn't something that's necessary for most kids, but if your young performer is working a lot, then a reel can be very helpful because they give decision makers the opportunity to actually see their work.

Then you'll find some personal stats. We include the child's age, height and weight, hair color, eye color, and their size. Both boys and girls can list their youth sizes until they grow into adult sizes. Boys would then use their suit size and girls would list their dress size. If the actor sings well, their range could also be included here. Again, be honest about this. If your young actor sings in their school choir but doesn't do much beyond that, they're not really training to sing at a professional level, so maybe leave it off the resume. We take ages off resumes once the actor reaches 18.

Resume Headings

The bulk of the information on an acting resume should be devoted to two things: work experience and education. The two often go hand in hand, but experience generally carries more weight than education, so we lead with it unless the child has yet to land their first job.

Each work category needs to have its own section. As you can see on our sample resume, this actor has done some TV, a couple of independent films, an industrial and some voice over. There's also a category for commercials.

The Actor's Resume and Online Casting Profiles

No matter what kind of experience your young actor has, you always want to lead with the most impressive credits first, right at the top. By impressive I mean the hardest kind of work to get. In Chicago that usually means film or TV work. We also apply the "impressive first" strategy within categories. We want to list the most recognizable, and/or most viewed thing the child has done within a category first, followed by the rest. That goes for each category with a couple of exceptions noted below.

TV

We use a three-column format for listing TV credits. On the left is the show title, in the center is the kind of role the actor booked, and on the right is the network and director, which are listed together as a pair.

There are four kinds of roles that an actor can get in a TV show. The first is a co-star. We might see co-stars only briefly in the episode as they help move the story forward. This might be a kid that tells a teacher a bit of news, or a coach that gives a short speech to a soccer team. Co-stars are sometimes referred to as functionary roles (because they serve a specific function in the plot), and will be on screen for a moment or two. They could have one or two scenes and will often shoot their role in a single day.

A step up is a guest star, which is a role that is more visible in the episode. The story of the episode might actually revolve around a guest star. These characters will be in multiple scenes and will likely shoot a few days or more on the show.

Some guest starring roles will come back for multiple episodes, and when that happens they are called recurring roles, the third kind of TV booking an actor can get. There are times when an actor is booked for a single episode, and the character is brought back for more as the series unfolds. This happened to me. I booked an episode in Season 2 of *Chicago PD*, then wound up doing many more through Season 4. When this happens, it's a nice surprise!

At the top of the TV role food chain are the series regulars. These are the actors that appear in every episode of the show.

Film

We also use the three column format when listing film credits. The first column is for the title of the project, the second contains the type of role, and the third is for the studio and director. There are only two types of roles in film that are worth including on a resume: supporting and lead roles. Most kids are going to be cast as supporting, though once in a while a film needs a child for one of their leads. When they're auditioning for a film, you'll be told what kind of role for which your performer is reading. The studio and director are pretty self-explanatory.

Theater

This category holds a lot of weight with decision makers in town. Chicago has a very active theater scene, and people want to know when an actor has worked in it. We list credits with the same three-column system. The first is for the production's title, the second is for the role (the character name) and the third is for the theater company that produced the show. Follow the impressive-first strategy here, too. Put either the biggest-name theater company first, or the performer's most visible role first.

The Actor's Resume and Online Casting Profiles

Industrials

Is this three column format beginning to look familiar? When we list industrials we use the first column for the name of the company that paid for the project, the second for role we did (not a character name, a literal role like employee or student), and the third for the production company that produced the project. Sometimes companies have their own in-house video production arm, and in those cases we just note that as "WhateverCo In-House". As you list credits, there's really no need to prioritize them because there's hardly an industrial project out there that's going to be recognized by decision makers.

Once an actor has a lot of industrial credits, they skip listing the roles and production company name, leaving the company names arranged in a visually pleasing way, like this:

McDowell's	FireTires	Smart Device	Rainbow Water Park
RealCo.	Hatfield's	TacoTwosdays	Cimba Insurance
String 'N More	Siesta Fields	Ranger Supply	Dairy Solutions

Voice Over

Some people will tell you not to include VO work on a resume because it has little to do with acting. I would disagree that it's not acting. It's true that many professional actors don't pursue VO, and as such, they don't let people know they can do it. If a young actor isn't pursuing this kind of work, you can absolutely leave it off. But if you have some credits to list, follow the "impressive first" strategy here as well. If you've got two or three jobs for lesser-known companies and one from a big name, list the big one first.

The formatting for the VO category is a little different than the others. That's because voice over jobs come in all kind of flavors, but the two most common are commercials (spots) and corporate work (narration). When your young performer books a VO job, you'll be told what kind of job it is. If the job doesn't exactly fall into either category, like if your child is providing the voice for a toy or gadget, ask your agent how they want it noted on the resume. I would personally just list the company name under narration, but some folks might have other ways of doing it.

Commercials

Under VO is the commercials category. You might notice that there's no information here, just the phrase "Conflict list available upon request." On our resumes, we never list product names under the commercials category because of something called the conflict rule.

Imagine this scenario: The makers of Tide laundry detergent are casting their new series of spots, and your child is called in to audition. You're sent a script, your kid works hard on it, and they nail it at the audition. You feel great about their chances, and then you never hear anything from Tide again. Then, a month later you're watching TV and you see the spot. And the actor they went with looks just like your kid! And they read the script just like your kid did! You can't see an obvious reason why that actor was chosen instead of yours.

There are a thousand reasons why that may have happened, but one of the most obvious ones is that you listed a credit for Cheer detergent on your child's resume. The agency probably liked what

The Actor's Resume and Online Casting Profiles

they saw in your kid's audition and would have brought them back for a callback, except they have worked for one of Tide's competitors in the past. Unfortunately it doesn't matter how long ago they worked for Cheer, or that they didn't have a line in the Cheer spot, or (worst of all) that they were an extra in the spot. All Tide knows is that they don't want to hire anyone who's appeared in ads for their competitors.

Is this legal? Can Tide do that? Yes. In fact, it's sometimes applied by the actor's union as an exclusivity rule. In the chapter on unions I'll explain this in detail. But is it right? Well, yes and no depending on your point of view. The decision maker's position is that Tide wouldn't want your face associated with their product if it's already associated with a competing product. This makes sense, so you can't really blame them for ruling you out on those grounds.

The actor's position is more like this: "Hey, that Cheer spot aired a long time ago. It hasn't seen the light of day in years. The public would never connect me with both Tide and Cheer, so you're removing me from contention without any justification." All that might be true, but in the fast-paced world of casting, they have no way of knowing how old the Cheer spot is, and certainly aren't going to take the time to find out.

There are a lot of other people who can take your child's place on the audition schedule, so it's much easier for casting to just take them off the list. And this is assuming your child got to audition in the first place. Having Cheer on their resume might prevent them from even being called in for the audition. So the solution is to replace individual credits with the phrase, "Conflict list available upon request."

This implies that your child has worked in commercials before, and may or may not have a conflict with the product at hand, so if the advertiser is interested in them they should ask you or your child's agent about it.

You might have noticed that I didn't apply this logic to the voice over category. That's because people who hire voice talent usually decide whether or not to hire you based on an audio audition. They don't dig into work history. Even though it does happen, it's pretty unlikely that your child will be considered for VO work by the same people who hire them for on camera work, so feel free to tell the world about all the voice work your young performer has done.

Training And Special Skills/Interests

Finally we're down to the more personal categories: Training and Special Skills/Interests. This is a chance for kids to shine a little. Feel free to brag about what they're up to in their daily life, within reason. For training, list the name of the acting class and the name of the facility where the class was taken. Sometimes people also include the name of the teacher, but this isn't totally necessary unless you think the name might be recognizable.

The Special Skills/Interests category is where you get to have some fun, but do so while following a few rules. There's no format to follow other than to make it a short list of things your child does well. If they're big into martial arts, make a note of it. If they've been in ballet for years, list it. If they've accomplished something crazy difficult like holding the world record for cramming the highest

The Actor's Resume and Online Casting Profiles

number of packing peanuts up their nose, make darn sure that's on there. The more unique, the better.

It's a good idea to have a few practical things and at least one wacky thing. Think about including skills that producers might actually find useful. Our sample resume shows that this actor is proficient in Karate, she's musically inclined, and she's a gymnast. Those things help round out the picture the decision makers may have of her. The knuckle thing isn't there because we actually think it's going to get her work, but because it's memorable, and a huge part of the acting game is getting people to remember you. This, along with the Star Wars reference, can be good conversation starters.

You should only include things your child can actually do. If they ski, but only on the bunny hill and they fall face first every other run, they don't really ski. At least they probably couldn't do it successfully take after take. Be honest because if you say they can ride a bike without training wheels, but end up dumping the bike over and over at the shoot, they'll not only hurt themselves, but hurt their chances of ever working with anyone associated with that job again. Also, their agent will not appreciate hearing that a parent fibbed to get a kid a job.

A Big No-No

Speaking of being honest, allow me to sound off on a subject that raises my blood pressure. I'm occasionally asked to look at resumes by actors of all experience levels. I'm happy to give my opinion, and it makes me feel good if I can help someone increase their chances of getting work. Yet sometimes I see credits that just don't make sense when I consider the actor who handed me the resume. This doesn't mean the actor's lying, it just means the he or she (or their parent) is motivated by a need to look good, or maybe just doesn't know any better.

If an actor has been an extra (sometimes called a background player) in a commercial, film, or TV show, that is *not* resume worthy. Here's why: Anyone who fills out an online form and sends in a snapshot can be an extra. My wife's 90-year-old father, who has zero acting experience, training or even interest, can be an extra if he wants. If you can show up to work on time and bring some wardrobe options with you, you can be an extra.

This does not make you an actor. I'm not saying it's not legitimate hard work. Back in the day, I sat around plenty of holding areas and waited twelve hours to do nothing. I know that every extra job involves getting up early, spending a ton of time waiting to be told what to do (maybe with a bunch of annoying people) in an uncomfortable holding area, and often results in never making it to set. Sometimes, when an actor does make it into a scene, they even see themselves in the finished project! For this, you figure, it should go on a resume! No.

Resumes are for roles that your child had to audition for, and compete with other actors to get. Credits on their resume are hard-won. Getting them takes nerve, perseverance and time. It takes none of that to be an extra. So don't cheapen the credits they have by including extra work.

What if your kid was hired as an extra and was given a line? This is called an upgrade, and it's rare. If it happens, do a little happy dance because it means the job is now resume-worthy. But don't

The Actor's Resume and Online Casting Profiles

dance too long. There are different upgrade rules for different kinds of work, so it should only go on their resume if you're asked to fill out all kinds of paperwork. Check with your extra coordinator or the second assistant director to make sure the performer has actually been upgraded.

An Actor's Online Profile

Once you've got a resume put together, you'll want to open up accounts for your child at the major casting sites the industry uses. Then you'll input their resume information into their actor profile. All of the same rules and guidelines that I just mentioned apply, so the actual transfer should be pretty easy since you don't have to come up with any new information. The only thing that may require a little more work is an additional piece of their profile called the Size Card. You'll input basic stats like height, weight, and sizes, but there are also opportunities to list more specific sizes like their glove, shoe, and even hat size. Fill out as many as you know. No need to hunt down anyone's hat size if you don't know it!

There are currently three sites most commonly used in the profession: actorsaccess.com, castingnetworks.com, and castingfrontier.com. At first glance it might seem like their primary purpose is to allow actors to submit themselves for paying roles, and that is part of their function. But the industry does not necessarily use them in that way, or see that as their main purpose. Instead, casting directors use them to organize and run their auditions, agents use them to submit their talent for those auditions, and actors use them to be available for and sometimes execute auditions. You also may interact with them by submitting your child for projects on your own, but that usually involves a paid membership. Basic memberships are typically free. I'll let each site inform you about that since they're all a little different.

Actorsaccess.com is probably the most dominant site at the time of this writing. A look around the site can explain things better than I can here, but if you've never used it before, let's go through how it works.

An actor will register and maintain an account and profile on the site. You'll upload your child's digital headshots and use their resume builder, a tool that allows you to lay out your resume as you would a pdf. You choose your work categories and your layout and input all the specific work information. If your kid is represented by an agent, you'll tell the site who they are so they can include the actor in the agent's roster. Your agent will have to confirm that your child is, in fact, with their agency.

When an agent thinks your child might be right for a posted audition, they'll submit the child's profile. The casting office that posted the audition will gather all the submissions, look at each one, and mark the actors they want to see. If your kid is on that list, your agent will be notified and they will send you the casting notice. It'll have all the details about the audition and the job. You'll be asked to confirm or decline the audition, and if you accept, then you'll have your child audition by following the directions given.

We'll learn more about auditions later in the book, but in general there are three ways auditions are held: in person, in person virtually (videoconferencing), or self-taped. In the first case, you'll get all the details emailed to you and then physically go to the

The Actor's Resume and Online Casting Profiles

audition when it's scheduled. In the last two cases, you will likely interact with the Actors Access site to complete the audition, either by using EcocastLive, their in-house audition tool, or by uploading your self-taped audition file to their server.

Pro Tips

If you want to make these sites work for you, there are a couple of things that are pretty critical to remember. The first is that you need to have the correct notification settings. If you don't know about an audition, you're going to miss it. The sites allow you to customize how you receive your notifications, so choose a method that works for you. I recommend getting them by text and email.

The other important thing about your profiles is that you have to keep them current. When you get new headshots, upload them. When your child does a new job, update the resume. If their sizes change, enter them in the size card. Sometimes casting will give production staff access to your profile information when your kid books a job. Their size card will go to the wardrobe stylist, who may be buying clothes for the job. If they buy the wrong sizes, you will make them mad. Never make a stylist mad because they are in charge of making your actor look good.

The point is that profiles are front-facing to the industry. Think of it like a more important version of your favorite social media profile. The people who will be deciding to rep or cast your child will be seeing the profile repeatedly, so make sure everything is true and as current as possible.

Performers With No Experience

Since most kids typically don't have much work experience, their resumes usually consist of some very basic information such as their name, their personal stats, and maybe some information on the classes they've taken. When they begin working and credits start to pile up, the education section can shrink.

Without any work history, a resume is pretty empty, and that's ok. My very first resume was a haphazard mess of mistakes, useless information, and white space. If you want a look at it, I included it in *Acting In Chicago, 4th Edition.*

If you're feeling like your child's resume might look a little better if it had more information, you can do things like increase the font size, spread the content out a little, and try to beef up the education and special skills sections. Just keep the overall look nice and professional. We wouldn't include funny pictures or drawings, nor any additional information other than what I've described here.

CHAPTER 8

Agents In Chicago

Up until this point, everything we've talked about has been totally within an actor's control. Training, headshots, resumes and our online profiles are all things that are up to us. Finding an agent is also up to us, but the decision to represent us is up to them. There are ways to increase our chance of getting an agent, but first, let's clear up some myths about them.

It's common for people to falsely think that agents get actors work. Agents get their actors auditions, but the final decision on who gets hired is up to the client. An agent connects actors to potential jobs, but most often they don't have any influence over who actually gets the work.

Another myth is that agents "discover" actors and make them famous. This is absolutely not true in Chicago. First off, agents don't actively go out looking to discover anyone. There are plenty of actors looking for representation, so the agent doesn't have to look any further than their inbox to find new talent. That's not to say they don't approach actors once in a while. A friend of mine was doing a show and when her agent came to see it, she noticed someone in the cast that was interesting to her. After the performance the agent asked for the actor's contact information. This kind of thing isn't typical, but it does happen.

Secondly, the very thought of an agent discovering someone is a notion from old Hollywood. Any actor who's in the public eye has gotten there through a combination of work, perseverance, talent, and a little good luck. They were not discovered and likely became an "overnight success" after working for years. Having an agent in your corner is invaluable, but if you ask one what their job is, none of them will tell you that it's to make their actors famous.

So what is their job? In Chicago, they're the gatekeepers of the work. Clients that need to hire actors contact agents, describe what they're looking for, and the agent auditions the talent that are right for the job. Or, casting directors call agents looking for talent, and the agent sends actors to their auditions.

Once an actor has gotten a job, their agent negotiates pay, coordinates the logistics of the booking, collects payment from the client when the job is done and then passes the payment to the actor less a commission. From the time an actor gets the call for the audition to the time they get their check, all the information about that job will come through the agent. That's their job: to facilitate the work that comes across their desk.

It's worth noting the difference between an agent and a casting director, because it's commonly misunderstood. Agents represent actors, casting directors don't. A casting director narrows down the search for actors from the entire talent pool in their market (and sometimes nationally). In pursuit of assembling the best cast for the project, they audition actors represented by many different agents. As such, there's no duty to actors from the casting director's

Agents In Chicago

standpoint. Agents, on the other hand, do have a responsibility to work in the best interest of the actors they represent. Doing so involves being in touch with casting directors, and sometimes directly with producers if there's no casting director working on the job. Casting directors service clients, agents service actors. There is no such thing as a casting agent so don't ever use that term.

To compensate agents for their work, they're entitled to a fee. It's a percentage of what an actor earns for the job. Union actors pay a 10% commission on what the job pays, and nonunion actors pay 15%. This goes for everything except print work, which usually carries a 20% commission whether an actor is in the union or not.

While we're on the topic of agent commissions, there are a couple of things to keep in mind. Your child's agent can negotiate for the client to pay their commission, but most often we should expect our agent's fee to come out of our paycheck. Also, only the fee for the job is subject to a commission. If we're paid a little extra for travel or reimbursed for an expense we incurred while working, we won't have to pay a commission on that money.

Another misconception about agents is that actors work for them. Not so. Agents technically work for actors, and the good ones keep this in mind. But good actors think of it more as a partnership. A successful agent-actor relationship means that both are working toward a common goal. If the agent is doing their job, and the actor is doing what the agent suggests, the actor's career will advance and both parties win: the actor works and earns more, and the agent does too.

I mentioned the word "partnership". Agents will tell you that the actor needs to hold up their end of the deal. Training, keeping skills fresh and adding new ones, being reachable and available, and getting auditions submitted on time are all examples of this. Maintaining our online casting profiles is another important part of the actor's job. Some agents say having strong social media accounts are also part of the deal now, especially with young performers. That's a whole other conversation for a whole other book, but it can't hurt to have lots of followers on the platform of your choice. We'll talk more about social media in a later chapter.

The important thing for all newcomers to remember is that agents can't legally charge a fee to represent you. If you ever run into an agent that asks you for money before your child does any work, run far away from them. They're not legitimate. None of the agents I will refer you to will do this, but that doesn't mean that unscrupulous operators aren't out there.

Agents can, however, charge you for publicity services, like posting your headshots on their websites. This charge might come before you do any work, which is legal. The unions set a ceiling for that cost, but there's no one setting the rates for nonunion agents. The thought here is that if the agent is investing in a site and the talent are the ones that will gain the most from it, the agent should be allowed to recoup some of the cost. I guess I understand that, but my personal feeling is that having a company website is a cost of doing business. Many working actors have their own site anyway, which they pay for out of their own pocket. Why hit them up again?

The thing is, clients are looking at your agent's website every day, so it never hurts to have a presence on it. It can be helpful to an actor's visibility. In the end, whether or not you choose to pay these fees is your choice.

Agents In Chicago

Working With An Agent

Because every actor in town needs an agent, there is a healthy amount of competition for representation. Agents can be choosey about who they want on their roster, because there's an unlimited supply of actors (even young ones) and a limited supply of agents.

Actors hire agents for two things: their contacts and their advice. In addition to coordinating auditions and jobs, good agents also care deeply about what their talent do with their careers, and will tell you what they think if you ask them. You should take advantage of their expertise as much as possible, because most often your agent will know much more about the Chicago market than you will. Treat agents with respect as knowledgeable partners in your career.

In Chicago, there are two ways to work with agents. Actors can be exclusive or multi-listed. Both have their pros and cons. When it comes to child actors, most agencies prefer they be exclusive.

If you're exclusive with a talent agency, then you do all of your work through that agent, and you're not represented by anyone else. Even if you get a job from a source other than that agent, like if someone contacts you directly, you're obligated to tell your agent and pay them a commission on those earnings.

In theory, actors who are exclusive with their agents are first in line for auditions. If something comes up that's right for the actor, an exclusive talent should get that opportunity over one who's not exclusive. This is part of the exclusivity deal: work only with that agent and you get more opportunities. In this situation actors have a partner in their career, someone who works on their behalf to help them work a much as possible. This is what you want from an agent.

Sometimes agencies don't initially offer exclusivity to an actor until they're booking a lot of work through them. This is called "hip-pocketing" actors. Once they realize they have a valuable actor, they then bring up the possibility of becoming exclusive. Other agencies expect actors to be exclusive with them from the start.

There are two big downsides to exclusivity. The first is that not every talent agency participates in every area of the business. They might be active in commercials, print, and TV and film, but if you're looking for your young performer to do VO, you're out of luck. The other downside is that you're passing on the chance to work with the clients of other agencies. Some clients bypass casting directors by going directly to agents, and many are loyal to one particular agency. This is especially true with clients who often hire child actors, and very common in industrial and print work. The way around this is to be with a very busy agency that has its hand in a lot of work categories, and also has a lot of its own clients.

Agent Hopping

The other way to work with agents is to be multi-listed, which means that an actor can work with as many agents as will take them. This is less common with child actors, but still good to know about.

When an actor is multi-listed, their auditions will come from all the agents that represent them, and no single agent can claim that actor as their own. Being multi-listed means actors can work with as many clients as possible. Casting directors contact most of the talent agencies in town when they have an audition, so theoretically the multi-listed performer is covered no matter which agent

Agents In Chicago

they're with (and agents with multi-listed talent assume this). The more agents you have, the more work you can potentially have.

Being multi-listed sounds like a great idea until all your agents start conflicting with each other. Sometimes multiple agents get the call to audition talent for the same job. If you're with three agents, and they all decide to put you on the same audition, whoever calls you first gets you, making you spoken for from that point forward. If another agent calls your child in for the same project, you have to tell them the child is already on that audition. This tends to make agents unhappy. If it happens too often, some may just stop calling because the kid isn't available.

The other downside to being multi-listed is that there's really no advocate for an actor. When you're multi-listed, an agent will put your child's name on a long list of actors who are registered with their agency, and that's the extent of the relationship until someone in the office learns that they can book work. There's little individual attention paid to any multi-listed actor because there's simply no incentive for the agent to push any one talent unless the actor is truly right for the job. Agents sometimes figure you're covered by other talent agencies, so they don't always include their multi-listed talent in everything.

Working with multiple talent agents also requires multiple work permits for child actors, which we'll talk about more in a later chapter.

Which Is Best?

It depends. When you're new to the business, being with many agents allows you to get to know a lot of people. I was multi-listed for years. I learned what it was like working with each agency, and preferred some more than others. Through the process of auditioning and working through them all, I had good and bad experiences. I learned who paid quickly, who didn't, who fought for the actor, who fought for the client at the actor's expense and which agents seemed more interested in their bottom line than mine. It was a great education.

I could never get every agency in town interested in me but at one point I was represented by nine, which got to be too much. I found myself spending a lot of time saying 'no'. I'd get four calls for the same audition and have to tell three agents that I couldn't work with them on it.

Then there were times an agent had something for me on a day that I was already booked to work through a different agent. When this started happening a lot, I began cutting back. I took stock of my time with each agency and made some choices. I let the good ones know that I wanted to work more with them and became deliberately less available to the ones I didn't gel with. Incidentally, two of the agencies I dropped are no longer in business.

My son has had two agents in his career. One in Chicago where he got his start, and one in Los Angeles where we now reside. He's exclusive with each, though it's important to note that Los Angeles doesn't really do the multi-listed agent thing. That's a Midwest invention.

There are real benefits to being exclusive with an agent. An actor who is generally unknown should see the agent push them a little harder, resulting in a larger volume of auditions. That theoretically translates into more work. Also, I can't overstate the importance of having an advocate in the agent's office. It's one thing to be on a list, but a whole different experience when you call the office and people know who you are, and are interested in what you have to say. There can be a real working relationship that develops between exclusive talent and agents, which is to everyone's benefit.

Making The Choice

If you're multi-listed, how will you know when or if it's time for you to go exclusive with an agent? It's hard to say, but there are a few things to consider.

If an agent asks you and your child to go exclusive with them before you've worked with them at all, consider asking for a trial period so you can get to know them before committing. They should be fine with that, since they'll have the chance to get to know you, too. If they don't agree, then it's up to you to decide if you want to sign your young performer's career over to someone you don't really know. It could work out well, but you won't know until you try.

On the flip side, you'll run into agents who don't offer exclusivity to anyone. This isn't a bad thing, it's just a business decision they've made. One agent I spoke with said the agency decided not to work exclusively with actors because they can't guarantee that anyone, exclusive or not, will get work. They didn't feel right about locking an actor down without that assurance. You may not know right away which agents work like this unless you ask, but typically the nonunion agents skip exclusivity. I had great relationships with offices like these for years.

If you feel like your child is being given as many chances as possible to audition and work, the number of agents you have shouldn't matter. On the other hand, if you feel like you're being held back by committing to an agent when you could be working with more, then you should make a change.

You'll know when you're ready to be exclusive with an agent when you start to feel like you're spinning your wheels working with too many people at once. After you've done this for a while, you'll start to realize who gives you the best chance of working and you'll want to have a deeper relationship with them.

My advice is to look carefully at who you choose. If you and your kid have the ambition to work in TV and film work in L.A., then you know not to go with the agent who has never offered up that kind of audition. Make sure that your agent of choice has clients besides casting directors. If you sign with an agent that has few opportunities other than ones offered by casting offices, you're better off staying multi-listed.

Once you agree to go exclusive with an agency, you'll need to let all your other agents know about your change in status. How you do it depends on your relationship with them. Call the agents with whom you've been frequently and email the rest. Be prepared for all of them to be unhappy. No matter how much or little you've worked with people, no one likes to hear that an actor is leaving their agency. Simply explain that you're making a decision you feel is best for your kid at this point in time.

Do you have to go exclusive? Nope. Many child actors never go exclusive with an agent. If you and your child are comfortable working with multiple agents, stick with it. As long as you're both happy with the volume of auditions you're getting, then it's mission accomplished. But it's good to know that an alternative is out there.

Getting An Agent

One of the great things about Chicago is that our community of talent agencies is pretty diverse. There are large agencies with many agents representing hundreds of actors, and one-agent offices working with a small, core group. There are agencies that focus on working with minority actors, others that do only union work, and some only serve nonunion clients. There are agents that only do VO, some who focus on print and some that are full-service, meaning they work on anything and everything.

Whichever agent you're interested in, check their website to see if they prefer submissions through regular mail, or electronically. For young actors, here's the process step by step.

1. Submit their fantastic headshot (or snapshots) and brilliant resume to the agent along with a cover letter using whatever method they require. If physically mailing, use a large manila envelope so the headshot doesn't have to be folded. The cover letter should be short and to the point. You don't have to sell them on your kid, so no need to mention that your child always wins their school's talent show. Just keep it simple, like this:

    Dear Molly,

    I'm the parent of 8-year-old Emma, and we are looking to expand her employment potential in the Chicago market. I'm submitting her headshot and resume for consideration by your agency. I'd love to chat with about about how we can have a mutually beneficial relationship.

If you think there's a place for Emma in your talent pool, I can be reached either by email or by phone. Have a great day!

Sincerely,

Chris Agos

chris@actinginchicago.com

312-555-1212

2. Wait a month. This is the hardest part because you don't know what's going on and you're anxious for an answer. The agent could have decided your child wasn't right for the agency, or the submission could be sitting on their desk, lost in their inbox, or in a submission folder on some cloud server. If you haven't heard anything from them after 30 days, send another note, one that reads like this:

Dear Molly,

About a month ago, I sent you my daughter Emma's headshot and resume for consideration by Molly's Talent, Inc. I'm still interested in pursuing a mutually beneficial relationship with the agency, and would love to have her read for you. We're open to either in-person appointments, or self-tapes. If you're interested, feel free to get in touch. Have a great day!

Sincerely,

Chris Agos

chris@actinginchicago.com

312-555-1212

This follow up is a little different than the first one, but still hits the same key points, which is that you're interested in representation, and you understand that there's got to be something in it for both parties.

3. Wait some more. Resubmit every month for six months, keeping your tone positive and upbeat, even if it's your sixth email and you're frustrated beyond belief that no one's gotten back to you. After six submissions, assume that they don't have a place for your child right now. But you never know, you may get a call down the road.

Some agents have very little time during an average workday to look at all the submissions they get, so they set it aside and go through them every so often. Some do this twice a year, some maybe every quarter. That means you should expect some time to pass between when you send your materials and when you get a reply. You never know when they're going to look at your submission. If you follow this system, they'll have six chances over the course of half a year to see your name. Someone will eventually have a look at your stuff.

Most agents who represent young actors also do print, so if you're interested in doing that kind of work, explore that with them after the agent expresses an interest. Or, if your child already has a comp card (a collection of looks they can pull off successfully), send it along with their headshot.

Did you notice that the process I outlined did not include calling or walking into agents' offices? Agents don't like it when you do either. Remember, agents are working. They have things on their mind, auditions to put together, fires to put out. Calling them or walking in to their offices will not help your child's case. You want to be persistent, but not annoying. It's a fine line.

Open Calls

Sometimes talent agencies look to add to their youth roster by holding open calls. They'll post notices on social media asking for actors with certain qualities to submit. Sometimes they're looking for certain ethnicities or ages of actors. Reputable agencies do this when they feel like they have a hole in their talent pool. There is never an invitation to buy anything or subscribe to a service. It's just a situation where they're saying, "Hey actors and parents, if this describes you or your kid, submit to us!"

Open calls are fine and can be good opportunities to meet decision makers without much effort. But you do have to be careful. If you ever come across an agency that advertises an in-person submission event, I want you to be super skeptical of it. Look up the agency and make sure they have a verifiable history of representing actors in the Midwest. There are some businesses that are based elsewhere and exist more to sell you things than to represent actors, and they will come into town and rent space for an event.

At the time of this writing, the only live event I know of where talent agents are present simply to explore new talent and not sell anything, is the CAST Convention. The CastCon is an educational

Agents In Chicago

event founded by the owners of The Chicago Talent Network, a group of nonunion talent agencies. Full disclosure, I was a sponsor of their very first event in 2022, and I will likely be involved with it in the future. That's why I'm comfortable mentioning it here. Note that it isn't really geared toward young actors, so it's best to skip it unless you have an older teen actor in the family.

They Called! Now What?

Each agency handles actors who are new to their agency in a different way. Some take the time to get to know the actor before they sign them, some don't. When I was looking for representation, I ran into two kinds of situations: agents who want you to register with them, and ones who want to meet actors to see what they've got.

If you're told to register, your name will go on a long list of talent the agent represents. They'll ask you to fill out some forms, give them your headshot files and maybe meet a few people at the agency. Some agents do all of this through email, which means you may never meet anyone there.

The ones who want to get to know new actors are far more interesting. You'll be invited to their office for an audition, or the audition could happen virtually. Some agents ask prospective actors to prepare a scene or monologue, or might have a few scripts for you to read cold when you visit. Your audition might be recorded. Be ready for anything.

Your child's audition footage may be reviewed by all the agents in the office and if there's a consensus reached in their favor, they'll be offered a spot on their roster. Some agents work with new talent for a short period of time and seek feedback on how they do before signing them up for the long term.

My very first agent, a very nice lady who ran a one-woman agency, asked me to come in and meet her. I remember this vividly because I hit traffic on the expressway, missed an exit, and generally freaked out most of the way to the appointment. I even turned around illegally using one of those openings in the median for emergency vehicles. For all of my panic, the appointment went really well. I had approached her to rep me for VO. She didn't have a recording booth, so I didn't read any copy for her. We just talked about my demo, and about what kind of work I might be right for. By the end of the appointment, I knew a little about her, and she knew a little about me. I was ecstatic, because now I had an agent! The phone would start ringing with auditions and I'd be making money in no time!

My second agent sent me a postcard thanking me for my submission and asked me to drop by the office to register. It told me what to bring, and which days of the week they saw new talent. Today something like that would come via email. I was so excited! I had another agent! The phone would really be ringing now! I had double the agents, double the auditions, double the work!

There's a phenomenon that occurs when actors register with an agent, and it's called waiting. I waited a few weeks for my first phone call. That turned into a month. Then two months. Then three, four, and five. I was unraveling with frustration the whole time. Here I was, trained, ready and willing to go on any and all auditions either agent had for me. I was also still submitting to other agents, hoping to pick up a third. Once in a while I called to check in with both agents, who kindly informed me that they had nothing for me. Finally after nearly six months, my first agent called with an audition. I booked the job. The moral of the story is, eventually someone will reach out.

But What If They Don't Call?

No matter the agency, there's one universal truth about all of them: they're in business to make money. In order to make as much as possible, they need to have actors that are going to give them the best shot at booking work. Keep in mind that when an actor goes on an audition, they're auditioning against other actors who are represented by other talent agents. So not only is that actor competing for the job, but the agent is too. As a result, agents assemble a group of actors they think gives them the best shot at booking the most work.

Sometimes, the agent is happy with the group they have and doesn't feel the need to add any new actors. But the group is constantly changing. Kids move, switch agents, or otherwise become unavailable. When there's a hole in the talent pool, agents are more open to meeting new actors, but only ones that can plug the hole.

Let's say an agency works with a small group of about 100 actors. The group is pretty evenly split between genders, ages and ethnicities. But lately there's been a few high schoolers leaving the business. They were into it for a while, but now they've moved on to other things. Suddenly, instead of having plenty of high school kids to submit, the agency needs to replace the ones that left. The agents turn to the submissions they regularly get, but they only look for high school kids because they don't need anyone else at the moment.

This is good to know because so many actors and their parents take it personally when an agent doesn't call them. If an agent isn't interested in representing your child, that may not say anything about their headshots, ability, or talent. It might just mean they're filled up with kids who compete with yours. In our example, once the agency finds a few older kids, they call them in to read one by one. After considering all of them, the ones that stand out get the call to join the agency.

It's a good idea not to take it too seriously when agents aren't signing your young actor. This is one of those things that you can't control, so there's no need to spend time thinking about it.

Other Ways To Get Agents

Since we know that you need an agent, is there a trick to getting one? People find all kinds ways of getting representation. Rule number one is to be persistent. I sent my materials to an agency regularly for years before they asked me to read for them. My first time at the office, one of the agents said to me, "Oh, you're the guy who keeps sending me stuff. You don't give up do you?" I smiled and proceeded to read the heck out of whatever she put in front of me.

I only got the appointment because I was in a class with a guy who was represented by them, and after we became friends he offered to mention me to the agency. The more people you know, the more likely you are to click with someone who's going to stick their neck out for you. By the way, this only works if the person who recommends you is a trusted and experienced actor at the agency. Agents listen to actors who are credible.

Another way to get signed by an agent is to already have a career. If your family is coming to Chicago from another market and your child has been in the business for a while, you'll have a very good chance of landing at an agency that will take good care of them. Agents like to work with families who understand how the business works. That's also why it was a very good decision for you to pick up this book. It saves agents from having to answer many of the questions parents ask. Your agent will appreciate that you're well-informed.

Checking In

After your young performer has been signed up by an agent, whether it's their first or fifth, you want to be on their radar. We do that by keeping in touch, but doing so in a strategic way.

It's always good to have a reason to contact your agent. If your child is doing a show in school, or at a theater, let their agent know by sending a postcard or email. It's good for them to see that you're staying active. If your child lands a film or TV job and they're multi-listed, send a note to all the agents that didn't get you the job. Tell them where they can see your kid and when to watch.

When I was working hard to make an impression on new agents, I had a little trick. I used to call to double check the details on all my jobs before I did them. This showed that I was a careful actor who didn't want to make mistakes, and it gave me a great reason to chat with the agent. The idea is to stay in touch without looking like you're desperate to do so.

Each agent has a different policy on when, how, and how often talent can check in with them. There are agents that have an open door policy. Actors can call any time and drop by as much as they want. There are also agents who don't want you to call, email, stop by or even sneeze in their direction. When you sign up with any talent agency, ask what their check-in policy is so you don't wear out your welcome.

Act Like You've Been There Before

While you're working with your new agent, the number one thing to remember is to be professional. You're operating in the business world, even though it's a creative business. Part of being professional means being easy to reach. Make sure you're always reachable by phone, text, or email and let your agents know if you'll be away for a while. When you get a message, return it quickly. A good way to tick off an agent is to be unresponsive. Sometimes auditions come with very little notice and need confirmation of the appointment right away. Don't assume they can wait for an answer.

Being professional also means showing up where you're supposed to be and on time. If you need to drive to an appointment, parking in the city can be a real pain, so leave for your appointments early. If it's a virtual audition, you have even less of an excuse to be late. When an actor is running late to an audition or job for any reason, it's important their agent is notified. The agent will

Agents In Chicago

then contact casting or the client to inform them of the actor's delayed arrival.

When you're on set, be cordial and keep your kid focused, allowing them to get the job done in a way that will make the client call your agent and compliment their work. That's how actors get more auditions and jobs. In a later chapter, we'll discuss on-set protocols in more detail.

After the booking, some agents like you to check in with them. They're interested in knowing how it went, but they also want to know how many hours kids worked in case you went into overtime. Overtime usually means more pay, so they use your word of what happened on the set as the basis for billing the extra time. There are strict rules about how long kids can work without a break. If you're on a union job, keep track of how long the lunch break was, and how many of your wardrobe choices the client used if they asked you to bring any, since there are fees associated with that. These are all things that may determine the final amount your child earns for the job. If you drove to the booking and it was outside of the Chicagoland area, tell your agent your travel times and how many miles you racked up.

Don't wait for days to do this, get all the pertinent information to your agent no later than the day after the job. This is one of those ways to stay in touch for legitimate reasons, so take advantage. Some agents don't require this, so if you're not sure, just ask what they prefer.

Stay Available

More than anything, kids need to stay available to work and

audition. Nothing is more frustrating to an agent, and nothing will end the relationship faster than if your child is difficult to contact or hire.

Let your agent know when your child won't be available. This is called "booking out". Book out when you're going to be on vacation, have a big event at school that can't be missed, or are booked on another job. Some agents want you to book out for everything, even auditions. Others just want to know when you're going to be out of town. Check with yours to find out their preferences.

Missing School

Everything on this side of the acting world happens during regular business hours. You can expect auditions and jobs to happen from 9 to 5, Monday through Friday. If your child is in school, you'll want to check on their policy for excused absences. Private schools are usually a little more accommodating than public schools. Regardless of which school your child attends, they likely have a threshold for the number of days a kid can be absent without it impacting their grades, or at least triggering some uncomfortable conversations.

The best approach is to be up front with the school's administration and let them know that your child is involved in the entertainment business. As long as you have the proper permits to work (more on this later) the school should be fairly cooperative. It goes without saying that if the student misses work or a test, it's up to the student and their parent to make sure the work gets made up in a timely manner. Communication with the teachers and the administration is the key.

Some schools have fairly strict attendance policies and dole out consequences for what they view as excessive absences. To mitigate this scenario, it's helpful to keep track of the days and times your child is absent from school for work. There will be times when they miss an entire day of school, but often you'll pick them up an hour or two early. These shouldn't count as a full day absence. If you find your student bumping up against the school's absence limits, your good record keeping might show that the student wasn't gone the full number of days the school is claiming.

Payday

Once your child has done a job, it's okay to ask their agent how long they think it'll take to get paid for it. If the agent has a history with the client, they may be able to tell you whether the client pays quickly or not. This information will help when it's been a while and you're wondering where the money is.

Union actors have safeguards in place that pretty much assure they'll be paid within a month, although sometimes it can take a little longer. Nonunion actors can wait quite a bit longer, up to 120 days.

If you think about it, the money's got to go through several entities before it winds up in the actor's hands. The company who hired the actor has to be paid by their client, which might have to get a check from somewhere else. Once your agent gets a check, they'll pass one along to you.

We'll talk a lot more about getting paid later, and we'll get very specific about numbers.

AIC for KIDS and PARENTS — Chris Agos

The Party's Over

Is there ever a time for an actor to break up with an agent? Sure. If your young performer is multi-listed, and you've got an agent or two that you never hear from, why waste time and energy on them? You don't want to hit the break-up button too quickly, but if you've been holding up your end of the deal by keeping in touch, following their policies, and staying available for anything that might come up, you should eventually get some positive reinforcement. If you don't, do you really want to be with that agent?

When I was nonunion, I registered with a really exciting agency, but I just wasn't getting calls from them. One day I was doing some background work on a commercial in Wisconsin. I was part of a crowd scene and a nice lady was positioned next to me. We started chatting. I found out that she worked part-time at this agency. I mentioned that I was with them, and she looked at me funny.

She said, "Really?" Terrific. Someone who worked there just confirmed that I wasn't in their loop at all. I nodded and told her I hadn't been contacted for anything since registering. Aloud, she wondered why. I just kept shrugging because I didn't have a clue. By the time this exchange happened, she had worked with me the whole day and knew I was good on a set, good with following directions and a nice person. That was all she needed.

"Do you have any headshots on you?" I did, and gave her a couple. She eyeballed my resume, and explained to me why I may not have been called yet. "You're pretty young, and a lot of what we get goes to older guys. Also, it can just be hard for new people to break through. The agents have their list of people they know they

Agents In Chicago

can count on, so they usually just call in the same actors, especially if there are only a few spots available. If an actor does a bad audition, the agent just looks like they don't know how to do their job." She looked at me for a second as I nodded along with her reasoning.

Finally she said, "I'll see what I can do," as she stashed my headshots in her bag. The next week, I had an audition at her office. And not long after that, I booked a large client that brought a lot of work to the agency. From that point on, I was on their short list. I don't know who I bumped off of it, but I'm glad there was room for me.

I've said that perseverance is the key to being successful in this business. But there's also a time for a reality check. If you've got an agent who simply won't allow your child to play the game, you have the right to walk off the field. How long you wait before you do that is up to you, but I'd say that 18 months is a good timeframe. If it's been a one-sided relationship that whole time, I think you've got to be realistic and call it quits with that agent. There's enough uncertainty in this business, and you don't need it coming from someone who's supposed to be supportive.

There are other reasons to break up with an agent. One actor told me about an agent who used his computer skills more than his child's acting skills. The agency would call him when their Internet was down, or when they were having issues with their website, but they wouldn't call his kid in to audition for anything. He dumped them, and rightly so.

If you have problems getting paid from your agent, you should make a change. Good agents know that they didn't earn that money, your young performer did. It's reasonable that they won't cut your child a check until they get paid, but if you consistently have to wait five, six, seven months (or more!) for that to happen, you should dump them.

Most agents are terrific. All the agents I'll mention treat their actors with great respect. They are very responsible with every aspect of the business they run. They work hard for the actors they represent, and are very good at what they do. Keeping tabs on the relationship you have with your agent is just another part of your job as the parent of an actor, because things don't always go the way they should.

Managers

Actors can also be represented by a talent manager. For decades, managers stayed on the coasts and didn't have a presence in the Midwest. But the Internet and global nature of casting is slowly changing that, so it's worth knowing a little about them.

Managers differ from agents in a couple of ways. Generally, a manager is supposed to be involved in the long term planning of an actor's career. Like agents, they may secure auditions for the actor, but they'll also look for other opportunities that may increase the actor's visibility to the market. Managers typically focus on the big picture as opposed to the short term. They are a little more hands on, and may have relationships outside of the Midwest that can help move an actor toward their goals. Managers try to work with agents together as a team, the idea being that the actor has two entities working on their behalf.

However, all of that potential comes with some caveats. There is no licensing process for talent managers, meaning that anyone can call themselves a manager. There is no governing body under which managers work, so there is no oversight. And many charge commission rates that are equal to, or even higher than, a talent agent. If you work with an agent and a manager, you'll pay 10-15% to each of them, meaning 20-30% of each paycheck goes out the door before it comes to the actor. Having two reps is expensive.

After a quick review of some of Chicago's agents, let's talk about auditions.

Chicago Talent Agencies

I've either worked with these agencies personally, or have friends whose children are represented by them. None of them paid me for my endorsement. Agents not included in this list may be great. Don't assume that agencies I don't mention aren't worth checking out.

Stewart Talent

If you've done any asking around about agents in Chicago, you've probably heard of Stewart Talent. It's one of the busiest talent agencies in the city, and also has offices in Los Angeles, New York and Atlanta. Stewart has departments representing actors for work in all areas of the business and has a department devoted specifically to child actors.

Stewart has strong relationships with producers, ad agencies and photographers. Clients often call the agents at Stewart directly for talent. For child actors, that means performers are competing only with other kids in the agency instead of with everyone in the city.

Turnover is very low at Stewart, both among the agents and the talent. I have been with Stewart for 25 years, and my son is also represented by them. It's rare to hear of an actor leaving the agency, and even rarer to hear of an agent leave. As an example, one of their VO agents just left after a 35 year career!

Stewart can be difficult for an actor to break into. As the big kid on the block, agents there are inundated with actor submissions and can afford to be very selective. That doesn't mean it's impossible to get them interested in you, but you do have to be persistent.

Stewart is a good place for seasoned performers to consider. Actors who have some resume credits are more likely to get a look than those just beginning their career. That doesn't mean you shouldn't submit if your child is new. Remember, you may fill a hole in their talent pool. Stewart mostly books union work but also works with nonunion performers on a limited basis.

Stewart Talent

400 N Michigan Ave, Ste 700

Chicago, IL 60611

www.stewarttalent.com

Paonessa Talent

After working in advertising and spending time as an improviser, agent and a freelance casting associate, Marisa Paonessa was encouraged by the actors she worked with to start her own talent agency. She did, and now represents over 200 adults, teens and kids for all areas of the business, both union and nonunion. Paonessa prefers to work with talent on an exclusive basis, which allows for closer relationships.

Actors wanting to submit should use the form on their website, and include a cover letter that's more detailed than the kind I talked about. They like to see some ambition, so tell them about what your child has been up to lately. If they've done a show or taken a class, the agents there want to know about it. They like seeing kids and their parents pursuing their acting goals. Paonessa reviews submissions regularly, and will reply if the young performer might fit into their talent pool.

Paonessa Talent Agency

1512 N Fremont St, Ste 105

Chicago, IL 60642

www.paonessatalent.com

Chicago Talent Network

CTN is Chicago's newest talent agency, but it was launched by two rock stars of the industry: Duane Sharp and Renee Ertl. They might have the most unique perspective on agenting of anyone in town. They're both experienced actors, and were also talent bookers at a busy talent agency for decades. No, that's not a typo. Between the two of them, they have over 40 years of experience in this market. They know their stuff and represent both adults and kids.

They have grown in a short time, and recently added MTN, or Milwaukee Talent Network for actors who live north of the border.

CTN has differentiated themselves by offering more educational opportunities than any other agency. They see it as their duty to help educate actors (and parents) on the ins and outs of being a professional in the industry. Seminars, meetings, and discussion groups are held often. And they've recently launched the Cast Convention, a trade show for actors and other industry professionals.

They expect actors to be on top of their game, though, so know your stuff before you approach them. Check their website for submission guidelines.

Chicago Talent Network

www.chicagotalentnetwork.com

CHAPTER 9

Auditioning In Chicago

Auditions are part of the process for almost any production. Very rarely do the producers know exactly who they're going to cast in a role before production begins, unless there are celebrities involved. If the cast requires regular people like us, there's going to be an audition.

What's interesting about auditions is the potential involved. When we're called in to read for a project we are putting ourselves out there for that commercial, TV show, or industrial. But in the Midwest, actors aren't the only ones who pursue multiple types of work. It's common for directors and producers to do the same. So when an actor auditions for the director of a commercials, in a sense they're also auditioning for all the director's other projects. The actor might not be right for the spot, but they might be perfect in the director's first feature-length film.

Remember the nice woman I met on set who worked at an agency that wouldn't call me in? Once she opened the door, the first audition I did for them was for a department store in Nebraska. I didn't book it, but the ad agency thought they could use me for a different project. They asked me to do another audition, this time for a local wireless provider, and I got the job. I did all their TV, radio, and print for a couple years. When we audition for one thing, we're actually auditioning for everything else on which the decision makers are working.

Two Ways To Audition

The audition hasn't changed much since it was invented. Actors are given some material to perform, we prep it, then perform it in front of someone who has the task of choosing the right people for the job. Recently, though, a pretty major change has come to the audition process, one that seems to have split actors into two groups: those that love it and those who don't.

Since ancient times, auditions have be carried out live and in person. Both actor and decision maker would occupy the same physical space, be it an audition room or a theater, to determine if that actor was right for a specific role. But the pandemic ushered in a new era, one where actors audition from home more often than they do in front of other humans. This trend had been slowly developing since about 2015, but wasn't widely adopted until it had to be.

Taping our auditions at home comes with some challenges. It's no longer good enough to just hope the child's performance is reflecting what's written on the page. Now we also have to be on top of the technical aspects of producing an audition that looks and sounds great.

The decision of whether to hold an audition in person or virtually usually rests with the client or the casting director. When you receive the audition materials, you'll also find out where your child will be taping. Sometimes, if the audition is in person and you can't make it, you can ask if they'll accept a self-tape. The answer won't always be yes, but it's still worth asking.

We'll go through the process for both in-person and self-taped auditions. This is important because at this point, the industry seems to be trying to figure out when to use in-person auditions over self-tapes, and vice versa. Casting directors in TV and film are fine with self-tapes, and they dragged commercial CDs to the party, too. Actors auditioning for VO jobs have been doing so from home for years. A lot of print work has cut back on live look-sees and have gone virtual. Industrial auditions still commonly happen in person, though not always.

What's clear is that self-taping takes some of the friction out of the process for those on the casting side, but it adds friction for actors. However you look at it, self-taped auditions are certainly not going away.

Auditioning In Person

Live auditions here work just like they do in L.A., Atlanta, or New York. Scripts are almost always provided ahead of time unless the scene is very short or doesn't have any lines for the actor to memorize. In either case actors will do their audition piece one time as they've prepared it. The person running the audition might ask for a couple of tweaks to the performance, and they'll do it again. Once everyone's seen enough, the audition's done.

If you're new to the idea of auditioning in a professional

AIC FOR KIDS AND PARENTS — Chris Agos

environment, let's start at the beginning. Your agent will email you the audition details. You'll be told what the project is, what role your actor is auditioning for and when their appointment is scheduled. You might also be given callback and shoot dates, which you should check against your calendar. If your young performer has a conflict with the dates, tell the agent. They'll either advise you to skip it or do the audition anyway to see what happens.

If you're not available at your scheduled audition time, they will likely try to get you a different audition slot, but may not be able to do so. You should consider this possibility before you reach out. Are you really not available? Try to make it work since rescheduling could mean losing the audition.

Let's assume you and your child are available. A script will likely be attached to the email from the agent. On rare occasions, scripts aren't ready until the day of the audition and the actor gets them when they show up. This usually only happens if the role has very few lines. Most agents and casting directors try hard to get actors their scripts with plenty of time to prepare.

When the role has no lines at all, these are called MOS auditions. MOS is an acronym that stands for "Mitt Out Sound," and no, that's not a typo. There's a bit of legend that explains why we call them MOS auditions, and it goes way back. The story goes like this: In the 1930's there was a German film director working in Hollywood. One day he arrived on the set of his latest movie to find the day's shot being set up. He noticed the audio crew was placing microphones around the set, and he stopped them. Yelling at them in loud, heavily accented English, he said, "Nein! Dees eez mit out sound!" He was trying to say "No! This is without sound!" But his accent made "with" come out as "mitt". It stuck and morphed into an acronym. To this day, everyone in the business calls a scene without lines MOS. Each letter is pronounced separately, like when you say USA. I have no idea if this story is true or not, but it's told over and over, so I assume it's at least partly based in fact.

Once you have all of the information your agent has, your actor should spend some time with however many scripts you're sent. This is for commercial auditions. If you're reading for a TV show or film, you won't be given multiple scripts, but you might be given multiple scenes from the project. These are also referred to as "sides".

The tough auditions are the ones where there's a lot of material and the actors are told to be familiar with all of it. That doesn't mean we need to memorize everything, but we should be able to do them while not having our heads buried in the script.

Usually, kids are only sent one script, though sometimes they're sent multiples. No matter how much material they're given to get ready for the appointment, the folks running the audition really only have a certain amount of time to get all the actors on tape. My advice is to make sure your actor is ready to do everything, but I wouldn't worry too much about being word perfect. An audition is not a test of an actor's memorization skills, especially if there is a lot of material to learn in a very short amount of time.

Wardrobe

Give some thought to what your young performer is going to wear for auditions. Look to the script for clues. Check out TV shows or commercials that have the same kind of setup as the one they're auditioning for and use what the actors are wearing as a starting point. For example, if the audition is for the role of a student at a private school, you might consider having your performer wear a plain polo shirt and khaki pants to suggest a uniform. You don't need to be exact, just do something that makes sense for what you read in the script. I once auditioned for a bank commercial, yet the role I was up for was that of a jogger. I showed up wearing my running clothes (new-ish ones, not old sweaty ones).

If you're not specifically told what to wear and there's nothing in the script to use for inspiration, there are some unwritten rules to follow. Kids are usually dressed casually, so you can go with that if you're not sure what the audition calls for. But there are different kinds of casual. There's ultra casual, where kids might be in dressed in what they'd wear on the weekend at home. There's nice casual, which could be something that makes them look a little more put together than normal (like pants and a nice top). And there's also upscale casual, which is a step up from there, maybe what they'd wear to an event like going to see a musical at a nice theater. Whatever you decide to do, just make sure the clothing choice is appropriate for the role and the situation the character is in.

There are a few things you should avoid. Stay away from clothing with logos or wording on it. These things pull focus away from the audition, something that we never want to do. We want them to pay attention to the actor, not the actor's shirt! If you're wondering, a little polo pony or sailboat on a shirt is okay.

Secondly, try to avoid seasonal items. Things like heavy sweaters or tank tops and shorts suggest temperature extremes which may or may not be present in the script. Stick with clothes that would make sense in moderate climates.

Finally, don't have kids wear anything that's striped or has bold patterns. Cameras don't deal with stripes on clothing very well. The reason is a bit technical, but comes down to how the chips and sensors in the camera process information. Stripes can sometimes produce an effect called a moiré pattern, which are ripples or waves moving on the screen over the striped piece of clothing. And prints just distract the viewer, so avoid them, too.

Grays and jewel tones look great on camera. Solid blacks and whites aren't a good choice. Red also makes some skin tones look funny, so most actors skip it and go for more subdued colors. Believe me, a wardrobe choice is never going to be the thing that either gets an actor a job or prevents them from getting it. But it is something that will add to the overall feel of the audition. They key is to make the actor the focal point, not their wardrobe.

Pro Tips For Live Auditions

Make sure to arrive to your child's audition on time. We try to make it to every appointment fifteen minutes early to find parking and read any additional information that might be posted in the casting office. Also, sometimes there's a short info sheet to fill out, or you could have been sent this ahead of time via email. It asks for things like the actor's wardrobe sizes and scheduling commitments (like other bookings) that might conflict with the shoot dates. If there are storyboards or other character descriptions posted, have a look at these, since they can be helpful.

AIC for KIDS and PARENTS — Chris Agos

After you're signed in and your actor has read what there is to read, have a seat and wait to be called into the room. This is a good time to remind your young performer of anything you talked about in prep for the audition. When it's their turn, their name will be called and they'll bring their printed headshot (if it's asked for), and their info sheet (if one is being used) into the audition room.

In live settings, kids typically audition without a parent present, though that is beginning to change. Today it's a little different and parents have the right to be able to see and hear their kids' auditions. But the reason they used to make kids go into the room solo was for producers to see if they can ignore the strangers, the lights, and all the other stuff on a film set and do the job even if their parents aren't there to encourage them. A set can only have one director. If a kid isn't able to do their thing without a parent nearby, then it'll make the day much harder for everyone since the parent will have to be the director for the kid, and the real director will have to work with everyone else. This is still a fact of production, but today if a parent wants to be at their kid's audition, they absolutely can.

When our twins were eight months old, we had them audition for a Fischer Price commercial. It was horrible and funny at the same time. As we sat in the waiting room holding our boys, a very nice casting person came to take them in. I think it was the first time they were ever out of our sight. It was weird for us, and apparently for them, because shortly after the door closed, we heard all kinds of screaming coming from that room. It wasn't long before the door opened and our boys were once again safe and sound and unemployed.

Let's talk about what you can expect from auditions for each of the different types of work available to child actors.

Commercials And Industrials

Auditions for these two categories of work are very similar. If held in person, they could take place at a casting director's office, or a client's office. Very rarely will they happen at your agent's office or at an ad agency.

At a casting director's office there will likely be at least two people in the room to watch the audition: the CD (or a session runner) and someone running the equipment. There may also be someone in another location watching the audition via video conference. At your agent's office it might just be you and your agent. At an ad agency, there could be a whole bunch of people watching. In any case, actors might be given some last-minute instructions which may or may not be completely different from what they were told before. In this business, minds change quickly and if there wasn't time to update the actors, they just do it at the audition.

Whether the audition is for a speaking role or not, they all pretty much run the same way. First, they need to get the actor on tape identifying themselves. This is called a slate. They might say "Go ahead and slate," or "Let's get your slate." When the camera's rolling the actor looks into the lens and says, "Hi, I'm (your child's name here)." Sometimes we're also asked to say the name of the talent agency that sent us on the audition, where we're based, and often kids are also asked their age.

The audition room will be arranged with the camera at one end, pointed at an audition area (which you can think of like a stage) at the other end. Sometimes there are very simple sets built. I use the term "set" incredibly loosely. If the scene takes place at a table, there will be one there with enough chairs around it to accommodate everyone in the scene. If specific props are needed for the spot, the casting director will provide it. Never bring in your own props.

Sometimes after the slate there's a little explanation about what the commercial's scenario involves. This is especially true when kids are auditioning since it's faster to make sure everyone is on the same page before taping begins. When it seems like the actor understands the scene, the audition will begin. Based on how the first take goes, the actor might be told to make some changes and incorporate them into their second take. Two or three takes usually is the most an actor will get, then they're free to go.

Every actor in nearly every audition is asked to do multiple takes. We can't possibly know exactly what the client is looking for before we go in, so we do our best on the first take and let them direct us for the rest. This is how casting directors try to bring us closer to getting the job. Sometimes they have kids do extra takes just to see if they can follow directions.

The one exception to the multiple-take audition model is a style of audition called the interview. Occasionally producers need to see more of an actor's personality than they would find by auditioning them the traditional way. This is usually the case when the character does some kind of simple, every day task in the spot. Anyone can color in a coloring book or toss a ball around, so it's easier for producers to cast these roles by seeing actors' personalities instead of their mastery of everyday skills.

Auditioning In Chicago

In an interview audition, they'll do a slate first. Then they may ask the actors a question or two, sort of a conversation starter. This isn't because they want to have a conversation, it's because having the actor talk a little makes it easier to get an idea of who the actor is. Sometimes the questions can be related to the spot like, "Tell me about your experience with baseball." Or they can be totally unrelated, like "What was the most fun you had last summer?" In any case, producers just want to get a sense of what kind of kid they're dealing with. Are they pensive, withdrawn and reserved? Or are they open, friendly, and exuberant? Obviously the questions will be age appropriate for the child.

Sometimes the decision makers are just trying to find people who sound like they'd be fun to work with. Other times, they're looking for the actor who will throw the water ballon with just the right attitude. Jobs like these are almost glorified print jobs, so a large part of the casting decision depends on the look they're after. But the interview can be as valuable, or more so, than the actor's look.

A few years back I had an audition for a furniture maker. The spot was set in a living room, and I was auditioning for the part of the guy sleeping on the couch. I'm not kidding, that was the extent of my role. I had to shift around a little when the family dog jumped up there with me, but other than that, my job was to sleep through the whole spot. Obviously, there wasn't much for the casting director to have me do except act like I was sleeping, but that's really boring to watch. So in place of that, they interviewed me.

I told a story about the day my dog ruined the canvas top on my convertible. We were on our way somewhere. My pup was seated in the front passenger seat and I was backing out of the garage. As

AIC for KIDS and PARENTS — Chris Agos

dogs frequently do when they're in cars, she got antsy and started doing her excited-dog-in-a-confined-space dance. She managed to bump the garage door remote on the sun visor with the top of her head, pressing the button to send the door down. I had the radio turned up, so I couldn't hear the door coming down, and the safety mechanism that's supposed to reverse the door when objects (like cars) get in the way wasn't working. So the door came down on top of my convertible as I slowly rolled backward. A nail head on the bottom of the door snagged the canvas and ripped a nice long hole in the top, which cost me six hundred bucks to fix.

Funny story, right? I later learned that it got me the job. One of the producers on the set told me that I didn't exactly have the look they wanted, but my story made everyone laugh, which made me the ad agency's favorite. That spot ran for three years and paid for a lot of stuff. So that silly little story was much more valuable than my fake sleeping ability. I still tell it whenever I can.

Voice Over

VO auditions used to take place in agents' offices, at ad agencies, or even at recording studios. Those were the good old days when voice talent actually saw each other. Now, we never see anyone because with few exceptions, everyone auditions at home. I miss the old days!

A home recording setup can be as simple as an iPhone and a closet, or as elaborate as a professionally designed and built booth with all the fancy tech that money can buy. You probably don't need anything high-end until your young performer is booking enough

Auditioning In Chicago

work to justify it. In the mean time, you'll want to have a quality setup that doesn't break the bank. That's probably a USB mic connected to your computer which should be running some free audio editing software like Audacity. For a complete list of equipment, grab the free VO resource guide at actinginchicago.com. And for a deep dive into the details, consider picking up a copy of *The Voice Over Startup Guide*, especially if you're new to VO.

Your agent will send you an email with the audition details and script. Follow the instructions to the letter. Some auditions want the copy to be read two or three times, some want you to label the file a certain way. When you're happy with your takes, you'll send an mp3 back to your agent.

There's almost no point in spending time on what an in-person VO audition is like. It's very rare for adult voice talent, and even more so for kids. Just know that if your child is called to an outside location for a VO audition, it'll either be at a recording studio or advertising agency. They'll be asked to do a couple takes of the script, which you might not get until you arrive, and that's about it. If there's anything more elaborate than that, you'll be told ahead of time.

Print

Live auditions for commercial print jobs are called "look-sees". Your agent will let you know where to be, when. You'll head to the location, where it's likely you will be joined by dozens of other parents and kids waiting to have their test shots taken by a still photographer. Sometimes it's a quick in-and-out, sometimes it's a little more complex and requires some explanation and setup before a shot is taken.

Honestly these kinds of auditions are happening less and less as photographers browse online galleries of young actors instead of bringing them in for a test shot. If you do find your child invited to one of these, just make sure they are wearing something that fits the job. That might mean bringing along a change of clothes when you pick them up from school. Lots of kids have changed in the car on the way to an audition.

TV/Film

Auditions for TV and film roles run the gamut from simple one-liners to multiple scenes. You might be sent a script that's a half-page long or ten pages. If the audition is in person, they're almost always held at casting director's office. If your agent has a taping room, you might read there, and they'll send the tape to casting. But for now, let's say your audition is with a casting director.

The big difference between a commercial audition and one for TV and film is the presence of a reader. The reader is an additional person in the room who reads the other characters' lines in the scene. They remain off camera, and are there for the actor who is auditioning to interact with. Your reader will most likely be a casting assistant. So if the scene happens between a student and a teacher, there will be an adult there as the reader, giving life to the teacher's lines.

Your young performer will do a take of the scene and then be given direction. They'll incorporate the new direction as best they can for the second take. If casting thinks they might need a third take, that's no problem. More than that, though, and time gets to be a little tight. When everyone's satisfied, you're free to go. The tape will be sent to the director by the casting office.

Self-Taped Auditions

As lovely as it is to see people face-to-face, the truth is that these kinds of auditions have largely been replaced by auditions done by actors in their homes. There's a lot to consider when we tape our own auditions, so let's go through some details about them in the next chapter.

CHAPTER 10

Self-Taped Auditions

It's fair to say that many, and possibly the majority, of your child's auditions will take place at home. For a while, self-taping was considered inferior to those held in person for a variety of reasons. But the pandemic pushed the entire industry to realize that this new way of doing things is more efficient for everyone.

As a result, self-taping is now a very important part of any actor's job. Casting directors want tapes that look and sound at least as good as what they'd produce in their office, meaning we not only have to think about the quality of the actor's audition, but also the look and feel of the video, too. So congratulations, you're now a video producer!

Your goal should be to put together an audition that looks and sounds as good as possible with the equipment you have available. To do this, you'll need a self-taping system that is affordable, reliable, and repeatable. We shouldn't have to reinvent the wheel every time a new audition comes in.

Thing is, there are a lot of ways to approach self-taping. Not every setup is going to work for everyone, which makes it hard to give specific advice. Plus, technology changes pretty quickly and the demands of the industry change with it.

With that in mind, let's start by looking at some things that will be universally true in every home audition situation. These truths will apply whether you're taping alone or with a digital audience. They'll also apply whether the reader is in the room with the actor (aka a parent), or digitally connected via videoconference.

Types Of Self-Taped Auditions

There are two types of at-home auditions. The first is what I call a standalone audition. This happens when you tape without connecting to an outside observer. It's just the actor, a camera, and a reader, usually a young actor's parent. Friends, acting coaches, or other family members could also be readers. In a standalone audition, readers are physically present with the actor doing the audition.

You'll tape the scene, and the file will be recorded onto your device, which could be anything from a phone to a fancy camera. You'll edit the file and send it off to your agent or some other decision maker, who will view it at a later date. You can have as many takes as you need to get your child's performance the way you want it because there's no one there telling you to move things along. In the end, the file will be viewed by the person (or people) doing the hiring.

It's also possible to have a standalone audition with a virtual reader. This happens when no one's available to physically read with the actor in the room. Most young actors aren't likely to be in this situation because parents will act as readers. But older kids, like teens, might occasionally find themselves in need of a reader. In that case, FaceTime, Zoom, or any of the other videoconferencing apps will come to the rescue and allow them to use a reader no matter where they are. More on this in a bit.

The second type of audition happens when you dial into an audition via an app like Zoom or EcoCastLive, and the audition is observed by someone else. Typically this will be a casting director, and they'll act as your virtual reader. This is similar to an in-person audition in that the entire thing is run by the casting person and is recorded on their end. The difference is that they are not physically in the room with you. They are responsible for recording, you don't have unlimited takes, and you don't have to do anything with the file after the audition is finished. You do still have to use your personal equipment and make sure the image is good and the sound is acceptable. When you sign off, your audition is complete.

The Look, The Sound, And The File

There are three things we have to think about when we do an audition at home: how it looks, how it sounds, and how it's going to be sent to and viewed by the decision makers. All three are equally important because they're like three legs of a stool. Take one away and the whole thing falls over.

The Look

The visuals of any self-taped audition should be completely focused on the actor. That means the viewer should be able to see the actor clearly and not be distracted by (or forced to look at) anything else in the shot. We accomplish this by putting our actor in front of a plain background and making sure there's enough light in the shot that they are seen in full.

We want the decision makers to focus on the audition, not what's on your bookshelf or down the hallway. In a perfect world, everyone would have about eight uninterrupted feet of plain wall they can stand in front of to do all of their self-tapes. In this world, you'd be able to paint it any color, it would be free from blemishes like cracks and picture hooks, and be in a quiet place that doesn't have any weird reflections or uneven light. Unfortunately a lot of us don't have a space like that, so we have to make one.

There are several options for temporary solid backgrounds. The cheapest thing to do is to hang a sheet against a wall. This is fine as long as the sheet isn't wrinkled and it doesn't have weird impressions coming from the stuff attached to the wall. You don't want your young actor to audition in front of something that looks like Han Solo encased in carbonite. Also, if you're going with a sheet, make sure to anchor the bottom corners so it doesn't float around if someone walks by.

One step up from this would be to buy a large piece of foam core, which is like really thick poster board. They're sold in various sizes at craft stores. Get the biggest one they have, which will probably be just large enough to do close-up shots. You will be able to order larger sizes online if you want the option to shoot wider. You'll need a way to hang it. Some people tape it to a wall, others put holes in the foam core and hang it on nails, still others use a tripod with a clamp attachment that is made to hold flat objects. Any of these is fine as long as the hardware is kept out of the shot. The downside to foam core is that it's not durable. It gets marked up and damaged pretty easily so you'll have to be careful with it. It's also hard to store because it's rigid, so it doesn't fold.

The next option is to invest in a portable backdrop. Some are collapsable or foldable, some are two-sided with a dark color on one side and a lighter one on the other, and some are solid rolls of paper or fabric that can roll out of the way when you're not using them. Sizes range from 4x4 squares of fabric to 8x13 rolls of paper. There's a lot of variation and which one you use will depend on how much you want to spend and how much space you have.

Many actors like relatively inexpensive collapsable backdrops for their portability. But the downside is that they're only good for fairly close shots. Most auditions require some kind of full-body slate. That requires a wider shot. If you've got a small background, the lens will show everything behind it as you widen out. There really isn't a great solution for this, which is why some people opt for a larger background that requires a support system of some kind. The less expensive ones come with one tripod, the pricier ones come with two and can support fabric or paper rolls up to thirteen feet wide. These systems are truly portable, and many come with a carrying case.

If you want something you don't have to set up and take down for every audition, there are permanent background supports that can be installed onto walls. They allow you to roll your backgrounds out when you need them and roll them back when you don't. Some even have room for up to three choices so you can use different backdrops for different moods. These are maybe not the greatest choice to install into a living room, but if you're shooting in a garage or home office they could work out great.

Whatever backdrop you choose, it should be a single color, or a very soft, unobtrusive wash of similar colors. There isn't one "right" color. Some casting offices tell you they prefer a blue background, others say they like a light gray. Definitely stay away from dark colors, which are tricky to light. I'd also avoid stark white backgrounds. You can't go wrong with a light blue, light gray or something in between. Avoid chromakey green, which is not flattering. Also, skip the metallic reflector. You don't want anything shiny in your background.

Now let's talk about lighting. It's very important that the audition is well-lit, otherwise no one may see it! The cheapest option for lighting is the sun. If you have a large window, it can be your primary light source. Some people face a window and put the back of their camera up against it so that as they face the window, they're flooded with natural light. This is the best way to use a window as a primary light source. Never, ever do it the other way around, where your actor's back is to the window. This will result in a silhouette on screen, making it very hard to see the actor.

Relying exclusively on natural light is risky because of, well, clouds. They move around and block your light, sometimes while you're shooting, which looks really weird on camera. And obviously if the only time you have to tape is after dark, the window trick isn't going to work.

Even if you're shooting near a window you'll probably need to even out the light a bit, so you'll need an additional light source. Most people start with a ring light. They're pretty inexpensive and

Self-Taped Auditions

allow you to mount a camera or phone inside them. These are great, but make sure you get one that's dimmable. It's always better to have more customization than less. The downside to ring lights is that they tend to reflect bright circles in actors' eyes, which can be a little distracting to some viewers. Also, ring lights aren't usually good for lighting large areas. They may be fine for auditions where you can stand in one spot, but if your young performer needs to move around a little, you'll need additional lighting.

LED panels are a great choice. They have become really sophisticated in the past few years with some that are multi-colored, run on batteries and come with remote controls allowing for adjustment from afar. These panels are sometimes sold in kits, and if you're going that route, think about getting a set of three. You'll be able to execute a three-point light setup, which can level up the look of the audition. Make sure you have a way to diffuse the light, though. Raw, untreated light from LEDs can be harsh, so plan on softening it with something as simple as a white shower curtain. Diffusion kits and other attachments which are made specifically for LED panels are also available.

For higher budgets, take a look at LED spotlights which can be paired with soft boxes and other light diffusers. These pack a punch, and are good for lighting up larger areas, but are pretty expensive compared to other options. Also, often they're sold without stands, so plan on adding one to your order.

Let's talk about your camera choice. You probably have a phone with a camera. If you don't, get one, or get a tablet. They're great, and can do double duty as an editor as well. Camera phones are completely acceptable at the moment, but may not be in the future.

AIC FOR KIDS AND PARENTS — Chris Agos

When the voice over industry started moving to a home-recording model, people could get away with recording auditions on their phones. That's much less true today. I routinely see "no iPhone auditions" in emails from agents. For now, using your phone to shoot an on camera audition is just fine.

If you have another camera option, it's probably a DSLR, mirrorless camera, or camcorder. These offer a lot more flexibility, but are pricey and make sense only if you already have one. Whatever camera you use, make sure it's mounted on a tripod. The shot must be stable, never handheld. And there is no such thing as a selfie audition, so if you're using your phone, always mount it so that you are shooting horizontally. Never shoot your auditions vertically.

Additional Things To Note

There are a few other things that can impact the look of an audition besides the backdrop and lighting. Treat self-tapes as if they were happening in person. Follow the same wardrobe recommendations mentioned earlier. Avoid using props. There is no need to create any kind of set, so keep things very simple. If the scene calls for the actor to be seated, try to use a chair that won't distract viewers. A folding chair is just fine. Have your young performer stand a few feet away from the backdrop. This can help avoid weird shadows on the wall behind them. You might not notice them when you're shooting but you'll definitely see them when you're watching the file.

Consider the actor's eye line. If you're acting as your child's reader, they should be speaking to you during their audition. Try to place yourself just off camera, close to the lens and roughly the

Self-Taped Auditions

same height. This way the performer will be looking just off camera. If there's more than two characters in the scene and you're standing to the right of the lens, have the actor place an imaginary second reader to the left of it. An actor should never look directly into the lens unless the scene calls for it.

If your child is doing an audition with casting on Zoom or a casting app, they'll probably be looking at the phone or tablet's screen during the audition. That's where the casting person will be, and they usually act as the reader. If the phone is mounted horizontally, their eye line might actually look pretty good since the lens will be to one side of the screen.

The other thing you can place to either side of the lens? The script. Yep, it's common to tape up scripts around the camera to help with lines that may be less than perfectly memorized. I do this all the time. Some audition deadlines are very tight, and depending on what else I have going on, I can't always memorize everything. So I tape it up in front of me, out of the camera's view, of course. Kids can also hold a script in their hands if they're unsure of the lines.

The Sound

It doesn't do any good to have a great looking audition if no one can hear it. Lets talk about some things to think about when it comes to sound.

The first thing to consider is your audition space. Ideally you want to shoot somewhere that has plenty of room to move around. It also shouldn't produce a lot of echoes. Avoid setting up in bathrooms, kitchens, and other places with lots of hard surfaces like tiled floors and walls. These rooms allow sound to bounce around (also called slapback), and it can sound kind of strange on camera.

Your recording device has a built-in microphone. It's better than nothing, but these mics are not your best choice. For one, their sound quality is lackluster at best. But the bigger reason to think about an alternative is that built-in mics will always be where the camera is, not where the actor is. This is problematic for auditions with readers. Typically, a reader will be closer to the camera's mic since they'll be standing just to the side or behind the camera. That means the actor is farther away from the mic, making the reader's voice the most prominent one on the tape. That's not what we want. The actor should have the loudest voice, not the reader.

I think it's worth the expense to upgrade your setup with an external mic. There are a few ways to do this. The least expensive and probably most effective option is to go with a lavaliere mic, which are wired mics that are worn on your clothes. They're sometimes called lapel mics, or lav mics. These can usually be seen in the shot, but work really well. They're inexpensive starting at around $35, but you do have to be picky about which one you buy. The cable needs to be long enough to reach your camera, because the other end of it is going to plug into your device's input jack. This presents another hiccup for people with phones that don't have jacks, but let's put that aside for a bit.

A step up from a lav mic is an external on-camera mic. These are sometimes made for specific products, like iPhones or iPads, but there's a greater variety of them made to work with DSLRs and mirrorless cameras. They tend to be directional, which means they pick up sound from one direction instead of anywhere in the room. This

Self-Taped Auditions

is good because they automatically amplify an actor's voice better than a reader's. They also free actors from the wire that comes with a lapel mic, and because they're located out of the shot, the mic won't be visible in the scene. Which ever you choose, make sure to look at the mic's connector. You may have to buy an adapter to make it work with your particular device.

The fanciest setups use the same mics that the pros use on set. This is by far the most expensive option, but will give you the best sound and most flexibility. You'll need a shotgun mic, a boom stand, a long cable, and it all has to connect to a box that will provide the mic with power before sending the signal into your recording device. This is overkill, but if you're an audio geek it's the way to go.

Your options are much more limited if you have a phone with no input jack whatsoever. I'd just stick with the included mic. But if you try that and don't like the result, you'll have to jump through a few hoops to use an external microphone. Currently there isn't a viable microphone that wirelessly connects to your device. There may be in the future but for now, you'll have to connect your mic of choice to an additional audio recorder. This means you'd be recording your audio separately from your video, and you'd have to combine them in the edit. Of course, this adds time and complexity to your process, and it's useless when you're dialing into an audition with an audience. So only do this if the extra hassle is worth it to you.

The File

Wouldn't it be great if doing an audition was as simple as pressing record, acting, pressing stop, and emailing a file? Unfortunately it is not that simple, and part of the reason is because there is no standard yet for saving, labeling, and transmitting an audition. Everyone wants something different!

Once you have an audition that looks and sounds great, you might need to edit it. Some auditions ask for one file, meaning that if you have a slate, it'll have to be included with the scene(s). If you're using a phone or tablet, it will come with an app like iMovie that allows you to do this. There are also external apps that you can pay for which will have more features. If you shoot with a regular camera, you'll need to get the footage into your computer to edit it there. You can use anything from Filmora to Adobe Premiere Pro as an editor.

Whatever software you choose, there a couple of things to keep in mind. It might be tempting to put a title card at the beginning of the file, or to put your young actor's name in a graphic somewhere on screen, but don't do that unless you're told to do so. Generally people want these files to be free from distractions, and that includes graphics and lower thirds. You can, however, use the "fade" feature that comes with pretty much any editor. It's nice to fade up at the beginning of a file, and fade to black at the end. It's also good to briefly fade to black in between multiple scenes. You can experiment with different kinds of transitions, but generally it's best to keep them as simple as possible.

Also, avoid applying any filters to the image. It's one thing if you need to do something simple like lighten or darken it, but stay away from doing anything that significantly alters the picture. This isn't Instagram. You want it to look as natural as possible.

When you have your audition edited, you need to know what

to do with it. Check the email or casting notice that came with the audition. There you'll find details about where the file(s) should be sent, how many to send, how it (they) should be labeled, and size limits. Some people want one file with the slate and all the scenes put together. Others want the slate and scenes saved as individual files. Some casting folks tell you exactly what to name the file, others don't. Some offices need you to limit the file size to less than 100 MB, others don't want files at all, they would rather you post the audition to Vimeo or YouTube. It's the wild west out there.

The important thing is to follow the directions you're given. Casting sites like Actors Access and Casting Networks have their own system for uploading files, so if the casting notice came through them, follow their instructions. Both sites make it pretty easy to submit, but of course there can always be hiccups. One of the most common is that the file size is too large. Fixing this can be a little complicated, and it has to do with how your device records video. You may have to dig into your settings and see if it's recording at a very high resolution or not. Some phones record at 4K by default, which is not what you want. This produces insanely large files that are not conducive to auditions. Stick with standard HD or 1080p, which gives great video quality without the nutty file sizes.

You can also define what file type your device saves. There are several movie file types: .avi, .mov, and .mp4 are the most common. I recommend .mp4, which is a good type for our purposes. Your editing software will probably allow you to convert your file type from one to another. You'll notice that the file size will adjust with them. An .avi will be larger than an .mp4. It's not important why this is, what's important is that you're able to take a big file and export it in a smaller format. If your editor doesn't have that functionality, you can use a program called HandBrake, which is a super effective and free downloadable solution.

Some agents prefer that you send them your file first, which they'll then upload after having a look. In that case, you'll need a way to transmit something that's likely too big to email. I use a site called WeTransfer.com. It lets you send up to 2GB for free, and it does so flawlessly. You can also save your files to a cloud storage system like Google drive, Dropbox or any other service and send your agent a download link.

Virtual Readers

What do you do if you can't get someone there to be a reader? You bring them in virtually, of course! This usually requires having two devices running (one to shoot and one showing the virtual reader), but you can get the audition done this way if for some reason that's the only way it'll get done.

When you bring in a virtual reader, make sure you're positioning them as you would a reader who is in the room. Put them off to one side of the lens, and behind it a little. The actor should be able to see them, but you don't want the second device right next to the camera unless you're using an external mic. Electronic voices seem to cut through even more so than human voices in the room, so make sure the actor's is the loudest the audience will hear.

Want More?

Visit actinginchicago.com for my free self-tape resource guide.

Self-Taped Auditions

It has some specific equipment suggestions for all budget levels. Bottom line, there's no reason why you can't produce an audition that looks and sounds great. But if for some reason you can't, pay a taping facility to make sure your tape looks and sounds a good as possible. Most acting schools will offer this service, so call around to find the one closest to you.

Chapter 11

Callbacks In Chicago

The organizers of nearly every audition plan for a second one, called a callback. Not everyone gets to do the callback. It's reserved for the actors who seem most right for the job based on what they did in the first audition. Sometimes only two or three actors are called back. Other times, seemingly everyone in town makes the callback list. We call this an "allback", and it simply means the client hasn't a clue what they're looking for.

Most often a good number of actors are seen a second time, maybe a third of those on the first audition. The only kind of work that almost never has a callback is voice over. In all my time as a voice talent, I've done maybe two of them. My son has done only one.

A callback works in much the same way as the first audition. They can be virtual or held in person. Lately it's been more common to have a callback in-person. Usually actors will perform the same script, though once in a while they switch things up. I've been in commercial callbacks reading a revised version of the script I did at the first audition, or even a completely different one. You can expect more people to watch the callback than the first audition, either live in the room or online. These are the decision makers who will choose the talent after they've seen everyone.

Callbacks work just like first auditions except actors could be asked to do as many takes with as many variations as the client would like to see. When they ask us to do more takes, it usually means they're trying to see if they can get us closer to the performance that's needed for the spot. They also might be trying to determine how well we respond to direction, or they could even be looking for new and original ideas for the scene. Decision makers like versatility, so the more flexible and open to suggestions we are, the better.

Unless it's really short, actors are not expected to memorize a commercial script for the first audition. Casting offices usually have cue cards propped up near the camera. These will probably still be there in the callback, but since second auditions happen a few days (or sometimes even a few weeks) after the first one, you should encourage your young performer to have the script memorized by then. It'll just look better.

Callbacks At Home

All of the rules that apply to self-taping auditions also apply to virtual callbacks. Most often, a self-tape callback simply means you're taping with an audience. This usually happens via Zoom or one of the casting apps or websites. These callbacks involve setting up your self-tape environment, logging in at your scheduled time and doing the audition in front of casting and possibly the client. I have done Zoom callbacks with one person on the other end, and I've also done them with over ten people watching. Be ready for anything. One benefit of this situation is that you don't have to record these or send files, the person on the other end records the session.

I am all about setting things up to my benefit and comfort during these callbacks. I do what I can to make sure I have everything I need. I tape up scripts or make sure I have them close by, I have water within easy reach, and I'll crank up the air conditioning if need be. The great thing about auditioning from home is that you can take possession of the situation and make it whatever your child needs. Do they have a special furry friend that comforts them? Have it nearby, though if the furry friend is real and not stuffed, maybe keep them out of the audition space.

A word of advice about callbacks in general: Suggest to your young performer that they start by doing what they did in the first audition. It's what got them to the callback, so it must have been on the right track. If the client wants to see an adjustment, they'll speak up. But at first, it's a good strategy for actors to go in with the same intentions as before.

Can We Work Now?

Once your child has done the callback, how long will you have to wait to hear if they got the job? It depends. It's rare that all of the decision makers are present and can, without approval from anyone else, choose talent right after they watch the last actor. It happens though, and if that's the case you could get a call that day. Far more common is when the tape has to be viewed by someone who wasn't there, but who also has a say in who gets hired. It may be a day or two (or more) before you hear anything.

Usually there's one more hoop you have to jump through before the job is officially yours. After the callback, the field of potential candidates is narrowed even further. The next call you get might not be "your kid got the job," but rather "your kid is on check avail." Check avail is short for checking your availability. That means that the client has put you on notice that they have first dibs on your child on the shoot date. Once you agree to the date(s) they can either book your kid, which means they got the job, or release them, which means someone else did.

Being on check avail means your kid is still in the running for the job, but it can also lead to some confusion. Let's look at an example. An actor, we'll call her Patricia, has been called back for a job that shoots on June 15th. Her callback happens on June 10th, and it goes really well. The next day, June 11th, she gets a call from her agent saying that the client, a software company, wants to put her on check avail. She confirms that she's still available to work on the 15th.

At this point, Patricia knows that she's on the short list of talent who are being considered for the role, but the client hasn't quite made up their collective mind about who to hire. On June 12th, the day after taking the check avail, her agent calls again, this time with news that a past client would like to use her for a job. This client, a well-known airline, wants to shoot on the same day the software company has her locked up. Obviously, Patricia can't be in two places at once. She has two choices: tell the airline she's not available and hope they'll move their shoot day, or tell the software company that she's got a firm offer for work on the 15th. Patricia's parents don't like the idea of passing up guaranteed work with the airline. They know there's still a chance that she may not be the choice for the software company's job, yet they know that telling them she's got another offer can cause them to drop her from consideration right away.

There's really no "right" decision here. Which way Patricia and her parents handle the situation depends on the agent's view and the family's own conscience. Some agents would say that the chronological order of things should be followed, which means Patricia should tell the airline that she's not available on the 15th. Other agents would say that since the software company hasn't given her a firm offer for the job, she's under no obligation to them until they do. The agent could place a phone call to the casting director to try to find out where Patricia stands on the list of actors being considered. Sometimes there are a lot of people on check avail. If that's the case, Patricia is less likely to get the job than if she was on a very short list. If the agent can find out where she stands, they can make a more informed decision.

Patricia's agent finds out that she's one of many kids being considered for the role, and after considering all her options, she decides that since she has a valuable relationship with the airline, she wouldn't want to jeopardize it in any way. So her parents and her agent ultimately handle it this way: the software company is told that Patricia has a firm offer for work on the 15th, and they need to make a decision about her, pronto. They have two choices: they can book her or release her. Who knows which way they'll go, but either way, Patricia's working on the 15th.

No Guarantees

If there's one thing you should know about this business, it's that there are no guarantees until we get paid!

Being on check avail is a promising step, but it doesn't mean your child has the job, so don't do the happy dance just yet. My son and I have been on plenty of check avails and been released more times than I can remember. My record with one casting office was 12 releases in one year. Once per month I was all set to work, then fired before I was even hired. My son had six of these in one recent year.

The chosen list of actors still has to reach whoever gets to make the final decision. Once that decision has been made, only then will a call go out to the actor who will be offered the job. If it's your kid, terrific, your agent will get a call with all the details. If it's not, your agent will get the other kind of call, the one releasing you from that date and your child's journey with that particular audition has come to an end.

Do you have to get a callback to get the job? Pretty much. Obviously if the client is planning on casting without a callback, you can book the job by auditioning only once. But if there's a callback and your child is not on it, chances are they're not getting the job. Everyone will tell you that they might, but I've never booked a job in that situation, and I don't know anyone who has. It's too bad, but clients want to see actors and work with them at the callback.

Alternative Audition Sources

Remember how I said that your child's auditions will come through their agent? This is true and it means that without an agent, you don't have a chance at auditioning for most of the work that's available to the actors in Chicago. You may be thinking otherwise, that you and your child can still get after it if you don't have an agent. That's also true, but let me talk about what's available to you when you decide to look for work in this way.

First off, remember that I'm only addressing auditioning for acting work other than theater. You can easily do all kinds of theater in town without having an agent. You might not have access to the big name companies, but plenty of others cast actors without agents all the time. What are your options if you're agent-less?

Facebook, Backstage, and Actors Access are some places people bring up when they talk about auditions they got without an agent. Some posts are quite legitimate on these platforms, and others aren't. You'll find people who are professional (or at least want to be), and who will respect you, your time and the process. You'll also find people who won't.

All I'm going to say about auditions you find on Facebook is that you never know what you're getting into. I have friends who have had good experiences with these auditions. Just be extra careful and ask a lot of questions before you agree to anything that involves your kid. Also, if your kid lands one of these jobs, know that no one is on your side to handle problems or conflicts if they arise. That's what an agent would do.

Backstage is another place to find auditions via their job board. They don't have a large presence in the Midwest, at least not as big as on the coasts. There are a lot of student productions and other projects where little to no pay is involved. I would tread lightly with these auditions as well.

AIC FOR KIDS AND PARENTS — Chris Agos

A better place to find paying work on your own are online casting services like Actor's Access and Casting Networks. These are sites used by agents and casting directors, so there's a multitude of legitimate auditions posted. Actors can submit themselves for a fee, and I've heard of a few people actually getting booked as a result. But still, unless you have an agent to back you up, you need to find out as much as possible about that job before you accept it.

Whenever you find an audition without the help of an agent, you should approach it with a fair amount of skepticism. That's not to say that all auditions you obtain on your own are going to be bad experiences, but you just have to wonder why the person who needs the actor doesn't call an agent. If it's a money issue, and they think they're going to have to pay too much if they call an agency, there's almost no point in doing the audition at all. Why would you give your child's services away for next to nothing?

Maybe to get your child some experience. You might figure that if your kid spends any amount of time on camera or behind a microphone, that will be valuable to them in some way. I disagree. It's been my experience, and that of others, that people who bypass talent agents are less experienced in hiring actors, and thus won't have anything to teach you or your kid.

Of course, there's an exception to everything. Sometimes legitimate projects look for "real kids" in the general public, meaning they bypass agents in search of kids who are not actors. The numbers don't work in anyone's favor at these auditions because so many people are on it, but you never know. Sometimes kids get jobs from them. Just do your research before you submit. Find out who the casting people are and what they've done in the past.

Another exception is when you know the person your kid is going to be working for. If your uncle Larry needs a video done for his company's website, do it. If you're approached to put your kid in a commercial for a family friend's car dealership, go nuts. However, remember that if you're exclusive with an agent, you're obligated to tell them about that job and pay a commission if you're being compensated.

Tips And Tricks

There are some things actors can do in any audition to help them snag the job. None of them will guarantee that we'll get hired, but none of them will hurt our chances, either. Incorporating all of them into your routine will help to bring a little order to what can be a chaotic process.

Plan ahead as much as possible. By that I mean you should help your child do their acting homework so they feel ready when their name is called. When you get your script, talk through it with them and rehearse it. If you don't know anything about the company or the product, look it up online. Same thing if you don't know the writer or director of a film or TV show. Watch an episode of the show if you can, or read the whole script if you can get it. Look up the director and writer on IMDb and see what else they've done. You can get a sense of what they like if you know their history. Simple things like this can go a long way towards being prepared.

Don't ever be late. Make sure you get your child's self-tape in on time. Once those deadlines pass, you're locked out of submitting. Sure, your agent can sometimes talk to casting and get the tape to them directly, but don't rely on that because it can't always happen. If you're going somewhere to do a live audition or callback, leave with plenty of time to park and get inside. You don't want to be rushed.

If your child has a callback, have them wear whatever they wore the first time around, and go with the same hairstyle. Sometimes clients remember actors by their shirt color, or by something else they noticed about them at the first audition. So don't give them a reason to ask, "Where's the girl with the braids in the brown top?" Also, encourage your kid to keep what they did in their first audition. The clients liked whatever they saw the first time, so help them remember why they called the actor back.

Chapter 12

Work Permits, Minor Trust Accounts, And Working Conditions

The State of Illinois requires all minors under the age of 16 to be granted an employment certificate (or work permit – the terms are interchangeable) before they're legally able to work in the entertainment industry. The State also requires the minor to have a trust account, where a portion of their earnings will be deposited and kept until they're old enough to claim those earnings as adults.

Illinois isn't the only state with such requirements for their young workforce. California, New York and other states also use the same tools to protect working children. Google will be the best place to get details of what's required to work in other states. Agents can also be a good source of information.

Be aware that if you live out of state and your child has to travel to Illinois for work, they'll have to satisfy its requirements *and* those of your home state. Same goes for Illinois residents who wind up booking something in, say, California. Some parents and kids wind up getting permits in three or four states at a time.

These requirements aren't just for parents. Producers also have to follow permit rules to legally employ minors. For this reason, everyone in the process makes sure that all the details are in place as part of the booking process. It's necessary to get these items taken care of before a child does their first job. Not having them will prevent the child from working.

Employment Certificates

The Illinois State Department of Labor issues employment certificates. There are various representatives around the state who handle applications. Your child's agent may send you to one of them. Some larger schools have a counselor or secretary act as a department representative.

The application process involves an in-person meeting between the applicant, the applicant's parents or guardians, and a department representative. It used to be required to physically meet, but now virtual meetings are also accepted. Your child will have to be at the meeting regardless of how its arranged.

The State requires you to bring a bunch of documents to the meeting. They must be originals, not copies. The requirements include your child's birth certificate and Social Security card, a signed letter of permission from a parent or legal guardian stating that they're allowing the child to work, a doctor's note stating that the child is healthy enough to work, a letter from the child's school stating that the student's grades and attendance record is good enough to let them work, and finally a signed letter of intent from the entity hiring the child. This is usually a talent agency, but could

Work Permits, Minor Trust Accounts, And Working Conditions

also be the production company of a TV show, or an ad agency. You'll also need proof of a trust account for the child, which we'll talk about in a bit.

These requirements are pretty standard across states, but sometimes they change, so it's a good idea to look them up online when you're actually going through the process. Each state has helpful websites with more than enough information to help you get your documents in order.

At the meeting, the department representative will review all the documents you provide, and if they're satisfactory, will issue a permit. You might receive a couple of physical copies as well as an electronic permit. You'll have to show the permit to any prospective employers, so you'll send it to your agent, who will keep it to send to production companies as your child books work.

Permits are valid for one year and have to be renewed when they expire. The renewal process is the same as the one to get the initial certificate, so you'll have to do the whole thing again. You'll gather all the documents and meet with the department representative every year your child is under the age of 16.

Multiple Permits

It's worth noting that the State requires a permit for every employer your child has. Talent agents are considered employers, even though they are not the ones making the decision whether to hire your child. This means that if your child has multiple agents, they're all considered potential employers, so you'll need multiple permits. Once you have a permit for a particular talent agency, your child will be able to work multiple bookings through that agent without having separate permits for each individual job.

This gets a little confusing so let's go through an example. Let's say your child is multi-listed with three agents in the Midwest. You'll need three separate permits, one for each talent agency. But if your child books five jobs for one of them, no jobs for another, and two jobs for the last, the three permits cover the child for all of those jobs. The certificates are to work with the talent agents, not each individual ad agency or production company out there.

This kind of rigorous process isn't in place everywhere. In California, for example, no meeting is required and there are fewer forms to submit. Your agent will have more tips on how to navigate your state's requirements when you go through the process.

Minor Trust Accounts

Blocked trust accounts are bank accounts that are sealed until their beneficiary (the child) is eighteen years old. Funds deposited to the account are legally the property of the child and no one else. As such, the only person who can withdraw money from the account is the child, but not until they reach the age of 18.

These accounts are commonly called Coogan accounts. They're named for Jackie Coogan, one of Hollywood's first child stars. He earned millions, but had to sue his parents to recover what was left after they spent most of it on luxury goods, cars, and diamonds. In 1939, The State of California passed the Coogan Law, requiring that 15% of a child's earnings be deposited into a trust account before any other entity has access to it. For example, if child earns

Work Permits, Minor Trust Accounts, And Working Conditions

$1000 for a job, $150 of it will be routed into their Coogan account before it goes to anyone else.

Most large national banks like Bank of America offer blocked trust accounts. You can also open an account online with the SAG-AFTRA Federal Credit Union if your child is a member of that union.

Wherever the account lies, you'll have to keep the account and routing number on hand because you'll provide it whenever your child books a job. The paymaster, or accounting firm that handles payment for the job, will need it to process your child's paycheck. And when you get a check stub, you'll see that 15% of the gross will be debited out to the Coogan account.

Your child's employer won't be the only one looking for that account information. The Department of Labor will want to see proof that the child has a blocked trust account in place before they'll issue an employment certificate. So this is something you'll have to take care of before you set up your appointment with the department representative.

When your child turns 18, you (or they) can notify the bank that holds their Coogan account that the child has legally become an adult, and they'll be able to access those funds.

On Set Rules

There are some specific rules the State has put into place regarding kids working in the entertainment business. These are designed to make sure the child is safe, and to prioritize their education over their work life.

The rules begin with the audition. Whenever child actors are auditioning, those appointments must be completed before 8:00 PM. Once a child is on the job, they must be accompanied by a parent or guardian on the set at all times. They must be given a 30-minute break for every five hours of work, and there must be at least twelve hours of turnaround time, or the time between they're sent home at the end of a day and when they come back for the next day of work. There won't be any overnight shoots for kids because they can't be scheduled to start work past 7:00 PM or arrive before 7:00 AM, although the production company can apply for a waiver of these rules under certain circumstances. During the summer months, when school is not in session, kids are permitted to work until 9:00 PM.

These are some of the main rules. If you're curious about others, the website of The Illinois Film Office is a great place to learn about them.

Let's now talk about what it's like to actually do a job.

Chapter 13

Being The Choice

After your child has done the audition, gotten the callback, and been put on check avail, they're booked! Now the real fun begins. If this is their first time working in a professional environment, it's good to know what to expect when they walk into work. Let's look at a typical scenario for each of the different work categories.

Commercials

There can be so much variation in commercials that it's hard to give you a set of circumstances you'd "typically" run into. Some shoots last a day, some a week. The job could be shot locally or out of town. You might have zero contact with the production company as the shoot approaches, or you might be on the phone with them quite often. We'll start with the most basic of situations and go from there.

Let's say your young performer has booked a spot for a grocery store. The shoot is local and they've scheduled your child for one day. Your agent will provide you with your location information and call time (the time you're expected to arrive on set), so you know where you're going and when you're to be there.

AIC for KIDS and PARENTS — Chris Agos

Before the job, sometimes the production company will call you directly. The wardrobe people might want to confirm your child's sizes so they can do some shopping. They may also ask you to bring some clothes to the shoot. You may get a call from the assistant director or whoever is in charge of talent on the project. Sometimes they just want to introduce themselves and see if you have any questions. Other times they have questions for you, and your answers might help the shoot go more smoothly.

In our example, let's say the spot is a cute little scenario with your child peering over the top of a huge bin piled high with apples. For the shot to work, they need to make the pyramid of fruit just the right height so your kid can look over it without having to bend over or go up on their tippy toes for any length of time. They call you to double check your child's height. Sure, their height is on their resume, but producers like to be as thorough as possible. That, and they know that sometimes the information on actors' resumes isn't as current as it could be.

This is also the time to make the production aware of any special needs your child might have. If they have food allergies, definitely mention them. Same goes for skin allergies, as the makeup department might have to order a specific brand. Producers will make every effort to accommodate needs if they know about them in advance.

In addition to a phone call or two, you should get a copy of the final script. Sometimes scripts are edited between the callback and the shoot, which means your child may have to learn new material. But in this case the final script is exactly the one they did at the callback. After you have all the information you need and the production company has everything they need from you, there's nothing left to do except show up and do a good job.

The morning of the shoot, you'll both be expected to arrive on time. It's important that you do, because shoot days are usually meticulously planned. Schedules are made well in advance, and many times there's little room for error. Specifically, the production company doesn't want the cast and crew to go into overtime. This usually happens when everyone's been there for more than nine or ten hours, after which they're paid time-and-a-half. The extra cost adds up fast. Often this can't be helped, but as actors we never want it to be our fault.

Remember my job for the furniture store where the only thing I had to do was sleep on the couch? I was late to that job. Just like the visit to my first agent's office, I thought I left with plenty of time to get there, but I hit some monster-level traffic. I started getting calls about fifteen minutes after my call time. The assistant director wanted an ETA on my arrival. The shoot was in an area of the city I had never been in and once I was in the neighborhood, I couldn't find the building. The next time he called I was close to the location. He wanted to know what kind of car I was driving so he could put a production assistant outside to flag me down when I drove by.

Eventually I found the location, pulled over, and let the guy park my car. I rushed in and got into makeup and wardrobe. When I finally walked onto the set I was almost an hour late. Everyone was nice about it, but the atmosphere was tense and I knew that it wouldn't ease up until everyone's focus shifted from the schedule to the work. By the end of the day I was forgiven, but I really could have done without the stress and anxiety. My lesson: when others are depending on you, make sure they can.

Let's assume you've arrived at the location on time. It's a sound stage the production company rented for the shoot. When you walk in, someone will tell you where to park yourself and your stuff. Usually when any member of the crew sees a child at a shoot location, they approach them right away to get them situated. But if no one greets you, find someone with a walkie-talkie clipped to their hip and they'll get you to where you should be.

Usually your first stop is an area to put your belongings. Don't be surprised if this area is different than that of the rest of the cast. Producers are required to provide an alternate holding space for children. For our example, say the stage has a green room. Hopefully you've brought your child's employment certificate along with you. You may need to show it to the set teacher if there is one. More on that in a bit.

You'll drop off your things and head to wardrobe. If they asked you to bring some clothes from home, they'll want to have a look at them. Before making a final decision they may have your child do a fitting, trying on a few options. Once the wardrobe people are happy, your child will head to makeup. This might be in the same room but won't likely be with the same person. A makeup stylist will attend to your child and will probably just apply some tinted moisturizer.

The stylist also might do your child's hair, or there could be a different person to do that job. You might wonder what kind of style your young performer should show up with. There's no hard rule, but there are a couple things to keep in mind. Some producers want kids to arrive with their hair completely un-styled so the stylist can do whatever is needed. More often, it makes sense for kids to arrive looking like they did at the audition or callback. That looked worked for the producers, so you can stick with it unless you're asked to do something different. If you're just not sure what to do, ask your agent.

After wardrobe, makeup, and hair, your kid will be ready for the day's first shot. This could take place soon after they're ready, or it could be a long wait. I've been rushed onto sets within minutes of being ready, but I've also waited hours between arriving and actually working. You never know what you'll find, so bring something that will help occupy yourself and your kid. Make sure you have some school work with you, because the set teacher may want to use it to help pass free time.

Set teachers are actual teachers, but their job involves more than making sure your kid does their homework. They are the child's advocate on set. They make sure you and your young performer has everything they need, and they make sure the producers are following the rules for breaks and dismissal times. They may want to sign the physical copy of your child's work permit if you brought it along. Union sets will definitely have set teachers present, non-union sets probably won't.

Whenever the crew is finished getting everything ready, you and your child will be brought to the set by a production assistant. They'll likely be your child's point of contact for the day. If you've got questions or concerns, they're the one to ask. On some jobs you won't have this kind of person, but usually someone makes it known that you're to come to them if you need anything.

AIC for KIDS and PARENTS — Chris Agos

Let's say they built what looks like the produce section of a grocery store on the stage. It probably looks better than any store you've ever shopped in before. In one area is a bin with the big pile of apples. There's a little platform for your kid to stand on right behind it, and stepping onto is allows them to peer over the top toward the camera, which is a few yards away.

On the platform is a bit of colored tape in the shape of a "T". This is your child's mark, and it's there to let them know where their feet need to be to make the shot work. The lights will be set specifically for them to stand on that spot, and if they're off even by a little, they'll be out of their light. It's important for all actors to know where their mark is and to stay on it as long as needed.

At this point your young performer will probably be visited by the person responsible for recording sound on the job. In my experience, it's almost always a man, though I recently had a female sound tech on a shoot! The gender gap in production is slowly closing.

Anyway, the sound person will place a microphone somewhere in their clothes. This usually involves securing the mic near the collar, and running the wires down the inside of a shirt, so it's all hidden. They will definitely want a parent's help, or at least presence, while this happens.

After the child is wired up, they'll wear a little transmitter somewhere, which will be connected to the microphone hidden in their clothes. About the size of a pack of gum, the transmitter usually sits on a belt or waistband in the small of the back.

At some point the director will introduce herself. This could happen before you get on set, but there are times when directors are busy with other things and can't meet the actors until they are ready to shoot. There might be some small talk, but pretty quickly the topic of conversation will turn to the shot. The director will likely want to do a little rehearsal. This is for everyone: the lighting folks, the camera peeps, the sound crew and the actor.

The many people standing around will all focus their attention on the set, but for different reasons. They'll all be doing their jobs, which all have something to do with the talent. The lighting guys will be watching to make sure no unexpected shadows or dark spots show up anywhere in the shot, the sound department will be listening for any audio anomalies (like if your child's mic rustles against their clothes), and the ad agency people (a.k.a. the client) will be paying attention to how the shot looks and how any lines are performed. The director is the liaison between the actors and the client. If the people writing the checks have any comments, they'll be passed along to the actors through the director.

Once shooting begins, it'll run much like the callback did. Your young actor will stand on their mark by the pile of apples and do take after take, listening to feedback given to them by the director. She'll be looking to get some different performance options for their client. Once everyone's happy, it'll be over. You'll be done in less time than it took you to get to the location that morning. All that prep for a half hour in front of the camera? Yep. Sometimes that's the way it goes.

This is a good example of how simple a commercial shoot can be. They can get even simpler. I've done commercial shoots in houses, where a bedroom or kitchen is the set. I once worked on a spot that was made in a park, and many of the shots were set up about as simply as you'll ever find. A camera on a tripod, one or two

AIC for KIDS and PARENTS — Chris Agos

lights evening out the natural light from the skies overhead, and that's about it.

Many jobs are much more involved. Usually there are multiple shots scheduled for one day. The crew has a lot of work to do in order to set each one up, which means a lot of downtime for actors. In fact, it's safe to say that there will be plenty of waiting on every job your child does. That's why I'm going to mention for a second time that you should bring something to occupy yourselves with. I know actors who bring video games, magazines, crossword puzzles and laptops. Most actors are glued to their phones all day long, anything to help them relax and pass the time. Kids should definitely have school work on hand.

The most complicated commercial shoot I've ever done was for a Midwestern state's department of tourism. The ad agency wrote a spot featuring a family traveling around and having fun. I was hired as the dad. Because all the shots needed to be at different locations around the state, the entire cast and crew had to drive to each new location for every shot. This meant doing what's called a company move, where literally the entire production and everyone involved with it has to pack up and move to wherever the next shot is located. This is complicated and time consuming. Our spot had three locations separated by hundreds of miles and took four days to shoot. It was a pretty sweet deal for us actors because if we weren't on the set, we were just hanging out in these fun places. We started off at an awesome museum, then headed to a theme park (where I puked my guts out on a roller coaster – not kidding), then finished up shooting in a huge underground cave.

Most commercial shoots are somewhere in between our grocery

store example and a grand tour of a whole state. Budget is always a concern, so no ad agency or production company would put anything in the schedule that isn't necessary. As your child books more and more jobs, you'll discover that some shoots are handled more elaborately than others. Depending on what the product is, you could have a bare bones crew with just a few people, or a large crew where even the wardrobe stylist has an assistant. There's really no way to predict what you'll run into.

Whenever you're working out of town, all of your expenses will be paid for by the client. For the tourism job, we were flown in, picked up at the airport and driven to our hotel. As the shoot progressed, we were driven around to each location and accommodations were taken care of every night. We were given cash for meals, which is called a per diem. If you're a union actor, a per diem when you travel for work is guaranteed. Nonunion actors may or may not get a per diem depending on what the agent negotiates. If you're not given cash up front, save all of your receipts to submit for reimbursement later.

In addition to being paid for the job itself, most clients cover just about every expense for the trip. There are, however, some exceptions to this. If you have to park your car at the airport in Chicago while you're gone, you may not be reimbursed for that. Also, you're on your own for anything you buy outside of meals. On the tourism job we had some extra time so we stopped at a cheesy t-shirt shop where I picked up a couple fridge magnets. Reimbursement for travel expenses also goes for when actors work out of town on industrials. Speaking of those...

AIC FOR KIDS AND PARENTS — Chris Agos

Industrials

This is another broad category of work that can have a ton of variation from job to job. Your child can be the only actor on the set or part of a large cast. There are jobs that will have very little for your kid to do, and ones where they'll have the most work of all the actors there. Some shoots will be overwhelmingly complicated, others as simple as can be.

In general, there are two types of on camera industrial jobs: narration and role-playing. With narration jobs, an actor delivers a script while looking directly into the camera as if he's speaking to the audience on the other side of it. Typically narrators are used to get a company's message across in the most direct way possible, by just telling the audience what the company wants them to know.

Role-playing jobs, sometimes referred to as day player jobs, feature two or more actors playing out a scene while ignoring the camera, like what you see in a movie or a play. Remember that industrials are videos produced for companies. A role-playing job might be two kids talking about the new touchscreen ordering kiosk in a fast food restaurant.

Very often you'll shoot an industrial at a location that's owned, or otherwise occupied by the company for which the video is for. These can vary widely. I've shot industrials in warehouses, greenhouses, paint factories, office towers, call centers, airplane hangars, science labs, boardrooms, courtrooms, doctors' offices, car repair shops and parking garages. I've even been flown by helicopter to a farm for a shoot. Most of the work you'll audition for is in the Chicago area, but sometimes you'll work out of town. I've worked in about ten other cities shooting industrials. Once your child is booked, you may have some contact with the production company, especially if the shoot involves travel. You'll know ahead of time if the job requires your kid to leave their home state. Something like that will never be sprung on you at the last minute!

As you work you'll discover that industrial shoots, like commercials, vary widely not only in location and subject matter, but also in complexity. I've had bookings where I was in and out in hardly any time at all. I've also been on shoots that lasted for days. There's really no "typical" industrial, but most of them are one to two day shoots. Producers are usually very good about letting kids and parents know if the day is going to go long. However, they'll make every effort to get you and your kid finished up early, and they'll also be mindful of the rules regarding how late a child actor can work.

With industrials, you'll probably be asked to bring some of your child's own clothes to the job. It helps to have a good selection of camera-friendly clothes. The instructions may or may not be specific, so try to have a reasonable sampling of clothing that would be typical for kids to wear. Boys should have one or two pairs of khakis, a couple pair of jeans, a few button-down shirts and a selection of t-shirts and polos in various colors. Girls should have the same kind of selection, along with a casual dress or two. You might also toss in a couple of hair accessories.

When thinking about clothing, stay away from garments with stripes and visible logos. Stick with Earth tones and jewel tones, and follow the instructions you're given to the letter. If they tell you to bring a selection of brown shoes, that means at least two pair. A few choices of whatever you're asked to bring is enough, no need to bring the whole closet.

It used to be that the majority of industrials hired makeup stylists for the cast. That's been changing as budgets are cut, so don't count on it for every shoot. You can ask your agent if makeup is being provided. If not, plan on bringing your own. Have a compact that matches your child's skin tone ready, just to knock down any shine.

After the job, you should try to get a copy of the finished product. This goes for every type of work, actually. Keeping copies of everything your child does can be important for a couple of reasons. For one, it's proof that they actually did the job in case the client doesn't pay. This almost never happens, but it's nice to be able to attach a screen shot to an email and say, "See, we did the job," if you have to. Secondly, and probably more importantly, you want to keep copies of your child's work so that you can eventually string together a couple clips for a reel. If you don't know what a reel looks like, visit Stewart Talent's site and check out a few, or you can visit www.chrisagos.com and have a look at mine. Basically it's a minute's worth of tape showcasing some of the work you've done in the past. When actors have enough work, they can have a commercial reel, an industrial reel, a film/TV reel, etc. Sometimes actors are hired off their reels without an audition.

Getting a copy, or a file of the finished production can be easier said than done. Commercials can be tough to get because ad agencies don't like to release their work until it airs. There's no telling when they plan on airing their spots, and sometimes even the producers won't know. It's not uncommon for many months to go by

Being The Choice

between shooting and releasing a spot. And some spots are never meant to be aired. Those are called demos, and they're made to sell an idea to a client, not to be aired publicly. Demos are almost never released to talent. Industrials can be tricky to get if there's proprietary information in them that the company doesn't want released.

You may not be able to get a copy of every job, but the only way to know for sure is to ask. Don't ask your agent, because that's not their responsibility. It's an actor's job to get our own files, so ask your contact person before you leave the set. They'll let you know who might be able to help get a file.

Since we're on the subject of what to do when a job is finished, let's briefly cover how actors get paid. If your child is a union actor, your contact person may or may not have a contract for you to sign at the job. If one is offered to you, sign it after making sure all the information is correct. Ask whether the production company wants an adult to sign on the child's behalf, or if the child should sign. Sometimes it depends on their age, sometimes it's how they've been instructed to do it.

If there's no contract on set, keep track of all the details and report them to your child's agent when you leave. With nonunion work, you'll likely have a payment voucher to fill out. Every talent agency has their own voucher, but they all basically require the same information: client contact information, job information, and date and times worked. It's important that you fill it out and have your contact person sign it when the job is over. You then have to get it back to the agent in a timely manner, because they'll use it to invoice the client for your child's paycheck. There's much more in a later chapter about how much your young performer stands to make from each type of work.

Voice Over

VO jobs, if you remember, are jobs where a voice is heard, but the actor is not seen in the project. Every VO job happens in a recording studio of some kind. They can take place in one of the large professional studios, or in your (possibly more modest) home recording booth.

Voice work is great for kids because it's very low impact in terms of time and commitment. It also doesn't come with any of the on camera hassles like making sure your kid is dressed correctly and their hair is done a certain way. In VO, no one cares what you look like, only what you sound like! And your child can make as much money (or more) as they can when they're in front of the camera while putting in a fraction of the time.

There are generally two kinds of VO work: spots and narration. Spots are just what you think, radio and TV spots. Most of these jobs are quick unless you're recording several spots at once. Narration is a longer form of VO work, and it can involve reading pages and pages of text for a video, documentary or TV show. As with commercials and industrials, your agent will tell you all the details about where, when and who your job is with. Kids mostly work on spots, but will occasionally have narration jobs.

While my son got his start in commercials, he's moved more into animation. It's an area of the business that's mostly recorded on the West Coast, though there are more and more opportunities for voice actors who don't live in Los Angeles. He's guest-starred on various animated shows, which means he's brought in to voice a character (or two) in an episode of a series. Sometimes he's brought back for more episodes, sometimes his character appears in only one. He's done jobs from our home booth as well as outside recording studios.

No matter the job type, you'll always head to a recording studio if you're unable to produce broadcast quality audio at home. When you arrive, you'll check in with the receptionist. They'll let the engineer know you're there, and you may have to wait while they get things ready for you. Your child may or may not be given scripts to look at while they're waiting. If you're handed a script, be sure to read through them with your young actor. Quietly read them out loud to see if there are any words or phrases that might be tricky. Everyone has a couple words that are hard to pronounce. For the longest time I got hung up on the word "cellular". I had to get over that really quickly when I was hired to voice a ton of spots for a cellular phone company.

Once it's time to record, your child will be called into the actual recording studio, "the room" as it's called. Parents are usually free to go into the room with children, but often it's just for introductions. There you'll meet the clients, who could be the ad agency people that hired your child, the producer the ad agency hired to produce the spot, or the folks who actually work for the company the spot is advertising. There could be one to as many as six or seven people listening in, either in person or virtually. You'll also meet the engineer, as well as the engineer's assistant if there is one.

Parents may be asked to hang out in the lobby once it's time to record. Your kid will be brought into the recording booth, which is isolated from the main recording room. If you're uncomfortable with that arrangement, you can always ask to be present at the time of recording, but it's unlikely they'll want you in the booth with your child unless they're very young. In that case, they may actually want you there to make sure your little one doesn't inadvertently play with something they shouldn't. Booths don't have much in them, but what's there is expensive!

When the child is in the booth and the mic has been adjusted to make them sound their best, they'll be asked to start reading through the copy for level. This is a rehearsal for the audio engineer. They'll tweak some knobs and dials to get everything sounding good. Once that's done, it will be time to begin recording takes. Your young voice talent will be directed by whoever is in charge. Usually it's a producer, but sometimes it can be the writer who wrote the spot, or some other person from the ad agency. Occasionally multiple people will direct.

Sometimes VO jobs use a technology called patching, which allows the talent and the producer to be in different locations, but still communicate with each other. Takes will be recorded at both ends. Patching software also exists for talent to use in their home studios. If your child does a lot of VO, it'll eventually become necessary for you to add it to your list of things to have at home.

The session will run the same way whether the clients are there in the room or if they're in a studio far away. Your child will do a take, it'll be considered and they'll be given some direction for the next take. The process will repeat itself until the producer thinks they have what they need. When finished, you can be on your way. There may or may not be a contract to sign like there is with on camera jobs.

As a professional voice talent, you want your child to show up as prepared as possible. There are any number of things that actors do to get themselves ready for VO jobs. Some do vocal exercises, some sing in the car on the way to the session, some eat an apple right before going into the booth, which helps to eliminate sounds associated with a dry mouth. They do these things partly out of superstition, and partly because their ritual works for them.

Personally I don't do anything special to get ready for a job, but there are a couple common sense things that will help make your child's time in the booth go more smoothly. First, always bring along a bottle of water. Many recording studios will have bottled water, but don't assume that it will be provided. Secondly, it's best if your child doesn't talk too much before their session. The muscles that allow you to speak can get tired if they're overused, just like any other muscle. When our voice is tired, it shows in our work. My advice is to do what you can to help your kid stay quiet for at an hour before their call time.

When a job is finished, ask for a copy of the final product. Try to ask the client for it within earshot of the engineer, because they need to get approval from the client before they can release it to anyone. There will be times when the answer will be no, but more often than not you will eventually be able to get the audio, which you can then use in future voice over demos.

Print

Of all the ways Chicago actors make a buck, print might be the simplest. In its most basic form, a print job requires an actor to be in

AIC for KIDS and PARENTS — Chris Agos

front of a camera for a little while and then go home. There are jobs that require more than that of course, but many are just that simple.

As always, your child's agent will let you know everything about the job. The agent will confirm that the sizes on file are still current. If they're not, give them updated numbers because in most print jobs, clothes that fit well are as important as the actor who acts well.

When you arrive at the photographer's studio, you'll meet the staff that will work on the shoot. You'll be shown to a dressing area, where you'll lay out any wardrobe choices you were asked to bring. You'll also find the wardrobe may already have for your child. At some point you'll meet the clients. They'll want to talk to your kid about what they'll wear. There will likely be a fitting, and photos will be taken of the child styled in each outfit so that they can choose which they like most. Those stills might also be sent to someone off site for final approval. After the final outfit choice is made, it'll be time for makeup and hair.

Print jobs are only about one thing: how an actor looks. So there's much more scrutiny of our physical appearance than in any other kind of work we do. During the shoot your kid will be told to shift their weight, stand up straight, drop one shoulder, lift their right hand, rotate their left hand, tilt their head one way (then another) and try a variety of facial expressions. Traditionally the photographer acts like the director and tells the talent what to do, but these days, with clients being able to see the images as they are created, input comes from many people. Most producers try to make the event fun for kids, so it should be a pretty lighthearted environment. Everyone will definitely be interested in getting the shot in a way that best serves the client's needs.

When the client gets the look they were going for, the job's complete. That could come after 100 images, or many, many more. The thing to remember is this: our job is to do what we can to give them what they need while we're there.

Sometimes, one photo shoot isn't enough to get it right. Very early in my career I was hired to do some product packaging for a company that supplies wedding products. Cake toppers, decorations, reception giveaways, stuff like that. They cast me as a groom, and the shot of me and my bride was to end up on a box of bubbles, the kind wedding guests use in place of tossing rice or birdseed in the direction of the happy couple.

The setup was really easy. I brought my own tux, which I owned only because it was a requirement for choir concerts in college (I think this is why I got the job in the first place) and they stood me and the wife in front of a pale blue background. We held hands and smiled, pretending that we were just married and by the end of the shoot, everyone was happy with the result.

A few weeks later, my agent called and said they wanted to shoot a second time. They liked what I did, but wanted to change out the model who played my bride. When I got to the second shoot, there was a different girl waiting to hold my hand, and we did the whole thing over again. About a month went by and I forgot about the job, figuring it was over.

It wasn't. My agent called again and told me they hoped the third time was the charm. I have no idea why they passed on either bride, but I didn't care because I was going to get paid three times. As far as I was concerned, they could marry me off to every model in the city. The third shoot was in a totally different location. It was outside in front of an actual church, whereas the second shoot had some kind of faux-stained-glass backdrop behind us. There was one little problem, though. This bride was at least two inches taller than I am, which the client didn't like. Apparently no one had done the math when they hired her, so the photographer had to come up with a solution. In order to make me look taller, they put me on her right side, which was in the foreground of the image. They also gave me something to stand on, boosting my height. The tricks worked, and this time they were even happy with the bride! The final image was on thousands of boxes of bubbles sold at Wal-Mart for a decade.

TV/Film

There's nothing quite like getting the call that your kid is the choice for a role in a film or TV show. For most of us in Chicago it doesn't happen often, and it's a special feeling. Unfortunately, doing the job is usually not as exciting as getting the phone call that you got it.

I haven't mentioned this yet, but I have a YouTube channel. It's got a lot of helpful content for actors, but one of the most-watched is a series of videos called *First Time Acting On TV*. It goes through every detail of what it's like to work on a TV show, step by step, and I highly recommend you watch it. It's a few years old but still very valid, and to this day I get DMs and comments from people about it. So search me up there and give it a watch.

I'm going to preface this section by saying that the industry is going through a transition when it comes to pandemic-related safety on set. For a while, there were very specific requirements for testing and masking, and shows had entire departments devoted to creating an illness-free bubble for actors to be in while they were working on the show. Those practices are constantly evolving, so know that you may have to test before you work, or you may not. Most productions also require actors to be current on their vaccines and boosters. That may change, so we shall see what sticks and what is temporary.

Working on a big budget film set is an exercise in waiting. Let's say your kid booked a role as a student in a PE class, and they'll need them on set for one day. As you might expect, your agent will have the details for you, but there's almost always a phone call or two from the production folks. You can expect your child's call time to be very early in the morning.

When you arrive, you'll be introduced to whoever is handling talent. It's usually a 2nd AD, or assistant director. It will be important for that person to know where you and your child are at all times because they'll be responsible for getting you wherever you're supposed to be. The first place you'll go is to your green room if you're shooting on a sound stage or to your trailer if you're out on location. And you could be there a very, very long time. Hours, in fact, without any contact from your handler, who might be busy with other tasks.

You'll also meet the set teacher, who may have a plan set up for the day. They may ask to see what school work your child brought, and they'll expect to occupy your child for at least part of the time they're with the production.

The call sheet, which you'll likely get the night before the job via email, will give you an idea of what your day will be like. You'll be given the most current one when you arrive in the morning, and

AIC FOR KIDS AND PARENTS — Chris Agos

on it will be all the information for the day's shoot. All the actors and their roles will be listed there, along with their call times and the shooting schedule. The sheet will have other information as well, like the weather forecast, the crew listing and a list of special equipment needed to shoot the day's scenes.

The day's sides will come with the call sheet, which are the pages scheduled to be shot. Look through them because the script may have changed since your child last saw it. Usually you're emailed script updates beforehand but if the changes are recent enough, you might just find out about them first thing in the morning by looking at the sides. Sometimes they add lines, or they may take some away. Just make sure your child is aware of any changes.

Let's say you're on location and you've been given a trailer for the day. In it will be your child's wardrobe. Don't feel like you need to get them changed right away. In fact, it's a good idea to wait until you're asked to change. If your call time is early enough, there might be time for breakfast, which is almost always served on large productions. Someone may come by to ask what you and your child would like, if anything. Feel free to order coffee! Lay off the sweet rolls, though, since you'll want to avoid a sugar crash.

Eventually someone will come to get your child into makeup and hair. They may or may not want them in wardrobe before that happens, so just ask if you're not sure. You'll be brought to the makeup trailer, where several stations will be occupied by stylists working their magic on the cast. You might find your kid seated next to the stars of the movie, or all alone by themselves. Be ready for anything. Often there's some chatting that goes on, so encourage your kid to be outgoing and have fun!

When the production is ready for your child, your handler will come get you and your child will be shown to the set, which in our example is a school gym. Once there, your handler will step back and your kid will be in the hands of the first assistant director and the director. Introductions will be made if they haven't been yet. (Here's a tip: if there's someone famous on the set, act like you've been there before and don't get all star struck. They're just people. This is more for the parents than the kids, I think.) There will be rehearsals, which are as much for the lighting and sound departments as it is for the cast, and when everyone's ready, shooting will begin.

Shooting will go just like any commercial or industrial. They'll do multiple takes, stopping between each one to make adjustments as needed. Your child's job at this point is to listen to the director and change up their performance as much as they're asked to do so. As a parent, you'll be asked to go somewhere you can watch. Sometimes that's with the set stylists, who are watching the shoot from their own monitor. You may be given a set of headphones so you can hear what's going on.

If they're shooting with only one camera, they'll shoot a master shot first. This will include as many actors in the scene as possible. After they're happy with the master, they'll move in for coverage, which means they'll shoot close-ups. There might be multiple cameras on set, which will cut down on the amount of time needed to set up new angles. Once all your child's scenes are shot, you're released and free to go home. You'll change wardrobe, hang it up where you found it, and be on your way. If you want to take off your child's makeup, the stylists usually have wipes or hot towels available.

AIC FOR KIDS AND PARENTS — Chris Agos

The process in our film example is the same if you're shooting an episode of a large budget TV show. But if you're working with smaller budget projects, you should adjust your expectations a little. There may be less people working on the set. There might be no one doing hair or makeup. There might not even be a call sheet if you're working with a very small and informal indie film production. If everyone's working for free, you'll be asked to bring your own wardrobe and maybe a prop or two. Chicago hosts productions up and down the spectrum, and when you audition for the role you'll know what kind you're dealing with.

The working conditions you're likely to run into while shooting TV and film depend largely on whether or not you're working on a union set. All large budget Hollywood-based productions are union, as are many smaller independent films.

Some ultra-low budget films sign agreements with the union, even though they really can't afford to pay union rates. The agreements make the producers promise to provide good working conditions if they cast union actors. They also allow producers to pay actors on a deferred basis. In these cases the actors aren't paid much unless the film gets distribution. This is a way for producers to be able to use union talent, and it provides more work for actors. When an actor works on one of these productions, they don't do it for the money. It's more about the experience and the footage for their reel.

If you work a nonunion film or TV project, there's isn't a set of rules the producer has to follow. That's not to say that all nonunion productions are going to violate child labor laws. There's absolutely nothing wrong with working on a non-union production as long as you're not a union member. Just be aware that you might need to advocate for yourself and your kid a little more.

The union plays a very important role in this business, and I think it's important for actors to know as much about it as possible. Let's talk about it next.

CHAPTER 14

The Actor's Union

Sooner or later, every actor mulls over the idea of joining the union. Whether or not to join is an individual decision, and I have my own view on the subject. But before I tell you what I think, I'm going to try to help you answer that question for you and your child.

Some Background

Until recently there were two unions, The Screen Actor's Guild (SAG) and The American Federation of Radio and Television Artists (AFTRA), that watched over actors who worked on camera and in voice over. But in 2012, the unions merged and adopted the name SAG-AFTRA.

The union's primary objective is to protect actors and their ability to earn a living wage. When it comes to kids, the union makes sure producers are providing safe working conditions and equitable pay through negotiating collective bargaining agreements. These negotiations result in contracts, which spell out rules that both producers and actors agree to follow on a job. They address everything from pay rates, to travel reimbursement, to health care.

The union doesn't negotiate for actors individually (that's done by agents), but for the entire membership. The contracts are the same ones under which all union actors work, and apply to broadcast TV, film, commercial, radio, web and industrial work. There are also union contracts for audiobook narration and video game voice talent, along with a few others. The union does not cover print work, although if there is a video component to a print job, that could be covered. Stage work is covered under Actor's Equity Association, a union that isn't relevant to our current discussion.

A lot of people outside the business wonder why SAG-AFTRA even exists. They hear about celebrities making millions and they assume that if actors make that kind of money, they can do just fine on their own. The reality is that the vast majority of actors don't make anything near those headline-grabbing fees, and they rely on the union to negotiate pay and terms that can help them earn enough to pay their bills.

The idea behind a union is to give employees (actors) the power to negotiate with management (producers) as one large group instead of individually. If you have a whole lot of people saying, "We need things to be done this way," that carries much more weight than if just one person takes a stand.

Many nonunion actors think that once they join the union, they'll have all the work they can handle because the union will see to it that they're kept busy. They assume the union works like a temp agency, finding work for actors and placing them in those jobs. This isn't true. Being in SAG-AFTRA does not guarantee that

The Actor's Union

your child will get work. They still have to audition for, and be cast in, the projects they do.

The union's responsibility is to protect members while they're on the job. In exchange for that protection, the union expects their membership to only take union work. Not all jobs available in the Midwest are union. The nonunion world is robust and not going anywhere. Before your young performer auditions for anything, you'll need to know ahead of time if it's a union booking or not. You'll see why later in this chapter.

Joining The Union

SAG-AFTRA requires actors to be cast in a SAG-AFTRA production before they can join. Since any union job is usually only open to existing members, actors have forever been frustrated by this catch-22 wondering, "If I have to be union to work the job, but I need the job to become union, how will I ever be able to join?"

This is a fair question. While producers of union productions sometimes just want to audition union performers, they're often open to seeing nonunion actors, too. Casting directors, agents and producers want to match the role with the best actor for it, and if a nonunion actor is the choice, so be it.

I broke into SAG like a lot of other actors, by doing a commercial. I was hired to voice a spot for Pepto Bismol. Back then I was doing all nonunion work, but I was with an agent who worked on both union and nonunion projects. She put me on the audition and I shocked her by booking it. My son also joined as the result of being cast in a commercial.

Actors can become eligible to join if they are cast in a principal (speaking) role in any union production. However, they can also join from doing background work. Doing so requires three days as a background actor on a union commercial shoot, something that most kids are unlikely to do. But it's good to know of that option.

Taft-Hartley

Actors don't have to join SAG-AFTRA immediately upon getting their first union booking. There's a federal law called the Taft Hartley Act that allows a grace period between when they work their first union job and when they have to join. Consider it a time to test drive what it's like to be a union actor.

Let's say you work your child works first their SAG-AFTRA project on June 1st. They're now in a new phase of their career. They are what's called "Taft-Hartley'd". Starting June 2nd they can work as many union jobs as they can get for thirty days without joining. However, once that thirty day period ends, the free ride is over. After June 30th, they must become a member to be eligible to work another union job. There's a special provision called an "OK-30" that will buy them another thirty days of work without having to join, but it requires approval from the union. You or your kid's agent has to call the union office and ask for it to be applied in your performer's case.

Most actors work their first union job and then don't book another one during their month of freebies. In fact, some wait years to join. This might be because they don't really want to join, so they avoid union auditions. Or it could be that the stars haven't

The Actor's Union

aligned for them, and they're still waiting to be offered their next union booking. It doesn't matter how long it takes between an actor's first job and the one that forces them to join. An actor's Taft-Hartley status never expires until they have a union card with their name on it.

You might be wondering how the union knows who works on what job. Producers are supposed to call the union office before they officially hire someone to verify that the actor is eligible to do the work. What makes you ineligible? Falling behind on dues. So if the union tells the producer that an actor is not eligible to work, that actor will lose the job before he even knows he had it. That's why you always want to be current on your child's dues. Not every producer makes that call, though, so the union relies on a second method of knowing who worked a job. Every producer who hires union actors has to file payroll information with the union. The producer's paperwork is used to make sure actors are being paid the correct amount for the job. The union gets a list of everyone who will be paid under the contract, and they check the names against their list of Taft-Hartley'd actors. If you want your young performer to be paid, there's no slipping through the cracks.

Once an actor is beyond their freebie period, they'll have to join the union before working their next union job. This can be tricky for a couple of reasons. First, you never know when that next booking is going to come. Let's say a producer decides to cast your child on a Thursday afternoon at four o'clock. That's great, except the job shoots the next day bright and early at 7:00. When the producer calls the union office to verify that your kid is eligible to work, they'll be told that your child is what's called a "must join."

That means you have one hour to join the union, because the office closes at five o'clock and won't re-open until 9:00 A.M. the next day. The producer will call your agent, who will call you and let you know both the good and the bad news. Your kid got the job, but they'll have to join the union before they can work it. Stressful, eh? As if that wasn't bad enough, the union has a substantial initiation fee. So now you have to come up with a good chunk of money on very short notice.

Most often, you're required to be physically present at the union office to join. However, for situations like this SAG-AFTRA has a grace period. Your child can work the job, but they'll have to join within the next five business days. What about the initiation fee? If you haven't saved up the cash to pay all at once, the union has a payment plan. Call the Chicago office or visit their website for details.

Becoming a union member is a rite of passage and a source of pride for many actors. To some, being in the union means that they've arrived, and they're really a professional. Before you consider whether or not union membership is right for your kid, it'll help to know what it's like to be a union actor, and how that differs from being nonunion. I'm going to break it down into two sections. First, I'll talk about the things you can expect from being a union talent. Then I'll tell you about what life is like as a nonunion actor.

Working Under A Union Contract

Being a member of SAG-AFTRA has a lot of advantages, most of which center on money. To begin with, the union makes sure that

The Actor's Union

actors are well compensated for their work. Union members have the opportunity to earn money while they're not even working. That's due to an aspect of the contracts called the residual system.

When an actor books a job on a commercial, film or TV project, they're paid for the time they spend on the set. That's called a session fee. Jobs are billed by the day, the spot or the hour depending on the project. On top of the session fee, union actors are paid a usage fee. In other words, producers are buying a license to use an actor's face or voice for a specific period of time. That usage fee is called a residual payment. We just call them residuals.

Say your kid is booked for one day on a commercial. The SAG-AFTRA commercial contract guarantees that they'll be paid a certain amount for that day, and no lower. This lowest possible rate is called the scale rate. Actors just say they're working for scale. The rate covers eight hours of work, so if your child works longer than that (up to the federal limits for underage workers), they'll be paid overtime.

In addition to the session fee, your child will be paid for the use of the spot. The amount of these residuals vary widely depending on where the spot runs and for how long it runs. Generally, the more people exposed to the spot, the higher the residual payments. I'll give you an idea of how much these payments can be in the next chapter, but you should know that residuals can be substantial.

The commercials contract also stipulates a session fee to be paid for each spot you do. So if your kid does five spots, they'll get five session payments, even if they're all shot in one day. And of course there will be five residual payments for them as they air. These have to be five distinct commercials. There are plenty of things that can be changed about commercials that allow them to not be counted as "new". Just an FYI.

The Conflict Rule

Producers of commercials can choose to use something called the conflict rule. By invoking the rule, the client is saying that they don't want an actor to pitch their product and a similar product at the same time. If you appear in a spot for Ford, a conflict means you can't appear in a spot for Chevy while Ford's airing your spot. In exchange for this exclusivity, the advertiser pays something called a holding fee, which is equal to the amount of a session fee. These fees are paid out over time.

This is a very important point for parents to understand. Clients take exclusivity seriously. If you don't honor your child's conflict by having them audition for competitors of the companies your child is already promoting, you could be in for a rude awakening.

In fact, if your kid did a spot for Chevy while their Ford spot was running and Ford found out about it, they'd ask you to pay back the money they paid your kid to not work for Chevy, or any other car company. And if Chevy found out that you had a Ford spot running, they'd try to claw back the money *they* gave your kid to not work for another car company. It makes more sense to avoid auditions for a competing product when you're getting holding fees.

Each time an actor gets a holding fee or residual payment, the advertiser is indicating that the conflict is still in place. This is only for TV commercials. There's no conflict in radio, or for certain online content.

The Actor's Union

You might think this is a little strange, that one company can dictate for whom else actors can work, but remember that we're getting paid *not* to work. And we get a holding fee for every spot we do. Five Ford spots means five holding fees in addition to five residual checks as they air. The money adds up.

If you think about it, the residual system is all about protecting the actor's image. As an actor, your face is really all you have. Residuals not only compensate actors for helping to market a company's wares, but also to discourage them from using our image too much, thereby limiting our future employment potential. This is another essential goal of the union, and one of the main reasons actors want to join.

Other Perks

The union contracts have several other benefits built into them. For example, often the agent's commission is paid by the client, not by the actor. So if your child is owed $1000, they'll get the entire amount instead of $900. Sometimes this has to be negotiated ahead of time by the agent.

Other perks for actors include a fee for wardrobe use. If you bring clothing choices to a job and your child ends up wearing them for the shoot, you get a little extra money for your trouble. Also, if for some reason you're booked on a job and it gets canceled within 24 hours of your call time, you'll still be paid in full.

I once auditioned for an on camera narration job for a beverage company. My agent called at 10:00 and told me that I was booked the next day. She called back at 2:00 to let me know I was released.

AIC for KIDS and PARENTS — Chris Agos

Turns out they decided I was too young and went with an older actor. While it was disappointing, I was still okay with it. Because they canceled less than 24 hours from my call time, I was paid for working a whole day, even though I was at home washing my car.

Finally, the contracts say that actors must be paid within 30 days of finishing the job. If producers pay late, there's a late fee. I've been paid in as little as a week.

Union actors also enjoy many other perks, most of which kids won't take advantage of. They include things like discounts on various services, loans and products, access to the union's own credit union, informative educational meetings, meet-and-greets with agents and casting directors, educational opportunities, and of course free screeners and downloads of movies nominated for best picture in the union's award show. Yes, as a member of the union, your child (or you, if you want) gets to vote and help decide who wins a SAG award. Pretty cool.

Benefit Programs

Union members have access to health and retirement programs, which is pretty important to adult actors. Kids might not care much about having access to health insurance, but it's possible for your working child to provide a health plan for themselves, or even your entire family. In some situations, that could be extremely helpful.

When any union actor is paid for their services, the producer makes a contribution to help fund the union's health and retirement plans, whether or not the actor is enrolled in the plans. The amount varies, but it's about 20% of the actor's fee for doing the job. This applies to both on camera and voice over work.

Actors have to qualify for these plans by earning enough money in any given year. Once an actor qualifies for the health plan, they can decide whether or not to participate, and if they do, they'll pay a reasonable quarterly premium.

One thing: actors have to re-qualify for health benefits every year. It's possible that your child may have health insurance one year, but lose it the next because they didn't earn the minimum amount to re-enroll.

Every actor who qualifies for the union's retirement plan is automatically enrolled when they meet the required earnings minimums. Our middle-schooler has a pension plan that will (hopefully) continue to grow as he keeps working. You can find the current minimum qualification levels, along with more details about these health and retirement benefits, on the union's web site.

All these perks, however, don't come free. In addition to paying an initiation fee of around $3000, union members pay dues twice a year. The amount is based upon our earnings in the previous year and increases as we earn more money. Dues currently begin at $227.42 annually plus 1.575% of our SAG-AFTRA earnings up to $750,000.

Working As A Nonunion Actor

Not everyone embraces union membership, and that's ok. The nonunion world has its challenges and perks, but more than anything else it's a great place to get an education. I worked for years as a nonunion actor, and learned a lot about the business from people who wanted me to do well.

Nonunion Opportunities

When an actor is not in the union, the work available is much the same as in the union world. Actors are needed for spots, industrials and voice over work. Nonunion agents get called for print work as well.

Nonunion actors might be hired to do similar stuff as their union colleagues, but they there will be some key differences. As a general rule, nonunion actors won't work for the large advertising agencies in town, or the large brands they represent. That's because those agencies have agreements with the unions that require them to use union talent for their client's work. Your child could do an industrial for one of these companies, but it's unlikely they'll do a commercial. There is plenty of nonunion work out there, though, so you never know.

Another big difference between the union and nonunion world is that there's no residual system and no holding fees. All nonunion work is paid on a fee-for-service basis. Actors are paid for their time on the job, and that's all. The producer owns the final product and can use it however they want, and for as long they want, without paying anything else unless a use fee has been negotiated at the time of the booking.

There are many stories about talent shooting or recording a project that airs for years, even decades, without further payment. The most shocking story I've heard is one told by Richard Schoen, an actor and voice talent who was, way back at the beginning of his

The Actor's Union

career when he sang non-union sessions, booked to sing on the "Save Big Money At Menards" campaign. If you live in the Midwest, you've heard this jingle. The chain of home centers is still using it today on TV, radio and in all their stores over 30 years later. They have lifted his performance many hundreds of times, each time creating a new commercial, and they have counted on his voice for nearly three decades to help build the brand. He was paid $250 for his work.

On the flip side, I know an actor who did a spot which ran for over 20 years. It was a union spot, so he was paid every 13 weeks that entire time. Makes sense to me, because the company sold a lot of stuff during that time thanks to that spot, so it's good that he was being rewarded for helping out. Let me tell you that no spot will ever run for 20 years again, so don't think that's the norm. But it's nice to be paid while they're in use, however long that may be.

In recent years, nonunion agents have taken a cue from the unions and try to negotiate usage fees for their talent. These fees are called buyouts, and they usually cover one or two years worth of use. So the actor gets a certain amount for the session and a buyout for the usage. Technically and legally, there are no product conflicts in the nonunion world because no holding fees are being paid.

That said, consider this scenario: Cole, a ten-year-old nonunion actor, does a TV spot for a local chain of family restaurants. The footage is cut up and used on TV and on social media. His agent negotiates a two-year deal that will pay him for both the session and use. The footage could show up anywhere for at least the next two years, maybe more if the company decides to renew the deal.

Cole's parents would like him to join the union if the opportunity presented itself, so he's with an agent that regularly sends him

AIC for KIDS and PARENTS — Chris Agos

on union auditions. About six months after the spot starts running, an audition for McDonald's comes up. Being perfect for it, Cole sails through the audition process and gets the job. In the interest of full disclosure, Cole's agent lets the clients know that he's got a spot running for the local restaurant chain. Upon hearing this information, McDonald's decides to go with another actor, one that's not currently pitching a competing product. This makes sense. Why would a major national advertiser hang the success of their brand on someone who's selling some other place to eat?

Sure, Cole's agent could have kept his previous booking to herself. But these things always come out. All it takes is someone from McDonald's ad agency seeing him in the other spots, and the pain begins. The fast food giant could make him pay back all the money he was paid. On top of that, once word gets around that his parents tried to game the system, he may not be be called in as often by Chicago's casting directors.

Nonunion actors have to think about conflicts, even though there aren't any in the official sense like there is in the union world. When I was nonunion I took whatever came my way, but I also knew that came with some risk. I was never in a Cole's position, but many actors will find themselves losing work because of their past choices. In case you're wondering, here's a very short list of big advertisers that cast in Chicago: Ford, Pillsbury, Gatorade, Sprint, Kraft, Proctor & Gamble, AT&T, Verizon, Home Depot, Miller, Budweiser, SC Johnson, Kellogg's, Comcast, Charles Schwab, DiGiorno Pizza, American Airlines, Hallmark, Bissell, Nike, Quaker Oatmeal, Subway, H&R Block, McDonald's, Best Buy, General Motors, Tylenol, and Volkswagen.

Independence

Nonunion actors have no one watching over the producer's actions. If there's unauthorized use, there's no way for an actor to know about it unless they come across it themselves or someone makes them aware of it. Unauthorized use means that the footage is used in places that weren't included in the original deal, like if an actor is hired for one commercial but the footage gets cut into many. In a situation like that, there's nothing you or your agent can do besides make a phone call to try to get more money.

In contrast, there are strict rules in place governing lifted footage that must be followed by producers hiring union talent. The rules say that actors must be paid for any project which features their voice or likeness. When you're nonunion, it's up to the actor to pursue fees for anything that's used for a purpose other than what was originally stated.

I don't want to give the impression that producers who hire nonunion talent are dishonest. The vast majority of them are great folks, but there are bad apples in both the union and nonunion world. The difference is, in the union world there's an organization you can go to with your complaint.

Remember my job where I slept on the couch all day? They lifted footage from that spot and turned it into a print ad, so the agency called my agent to ask how much they should pay for that use. My agent quoted them a price, and I was sent a check within a month. If they hadn't called and I found out about the print ad, the agency would have gotten a call from the union. If they decided that they didn't want to pay the additional fee, the union has an arbitration process.

When the difficulties with the client are bad enough, the union will issue a "do not work" order, preventing actors from working with that particular client until the order is lifted. Ultimately, union producers follow the rules because it makes more financial sense than to try and get out of paying actors. Nonunion producers can take the chance that an actor is not going to find out about a lift because there's little financial risk involved.

There are a few other protections that aren't available to nonunion actors. There's no wardrobe fee, nor is there a meal penalty. Overtime is usually paid, but sometimes it isn't. Also, when you're a nonunion actor you don't have access to health or retirement benefits from your acting work. The good news is that most nonunion agents have a cancellation fee in place so you're compensated for holding the time for a job.

I know a lot of this sounded like a bunch of gloom and doom, like I'm against the idea of being a nonunion actor. That's not the case at all. It was hugely beneficial for me and I learned a lot working with great people. Most of these jobs will pay well and your child will be paid in a reasonable amount of time. Most of the people you work with will be friendly professionals who want your kid to have a good experience. But I also want you and your child to have a realistic view of what to expect.

Making The Choice

So far, I've kept my personal views to myself, I've just stated facts.

The Actor's Union

Now I'm going to give you my opinion about union membership. After all, you bought this book to get some insight from someone who's been around a while.

Here in Chicago, the unions have a large presence, but there's also a lot of nonunion work. This is especially true of industrials and voice over, and as time passes, is becoming truer for commercials. Some actors have no intention of ever joining because there's enough work to keep them busy without having to be a member of anything but a health club. So it's not as though union membership is a prerequisite to being a working child actor.

One Way To Go

No one is born with a union card in their hand. I started out just like most actors in Chicago, by working in the nonunion world. So did my son. In fact, I didn't even know that the union existed until about a year into my career. At some point, probably by talking to other actors, I discovered there was this thing called a union and I wasn't in it.

That bugged me. I was in business to do well, and if there was a whole segment of it that I didn't have access to, I wanted to change that. So I tried to learn as much as possible about what it was like being a union actor. I started paying attention to the kind of work that I was getting. I was selling aluminum siding, or talking about food safety. Meanwhile, my union actor friends were booking jobs in car commercials and showing up in TV shows. It was frustrating that I couldn't access those better jobs.

So I decided to work on becoming a member. I made sure I was with agents who represented both union and nonunion actors, and

I let them know that I was interested in joining some day, so they knew to put me on any and every union audition that they could. This was my way of keeping my career moving onward and upward.

But there was a catch. I found out that once you go union, you can't go back. When you join, you agree to follow Global Rule One, which is that you don't do nonunion work. The benefits that come with being in a union like collective bargaining, residuals, health insurance and the rules written to protect actors came at a price. The union asks for your loyalty in return. If you make yourself available as a nonunion actor, you're working against the concept of being in a union, and if enough actors did that, the unions would up and disappear. Besides, why would a producer hire you through the union if you're available for less money as a nonunion actor? This made sense to me, but I was nervous to say goodbye to all the work that I had become accustomed to getting. It took me a little while before I was willing to make the jump.

I'm very happy that I made the decision to join the union. It's worked out well for me and my family. When the time came for my son to join, I didn't hesitate to sign him up as well. I just think the benefits outweigh the downsides. But this is an individual decision, so you should consider your child's situation and what you both really want out of this business before deciding whether or not to join.

Things To Consider

Enough about me and my kid, what about you and yours? Obviously, everyone has to decide for themselves whether it's worth the cost and effort to go union. You may want to consider a few things.

The Actor's Union

In the Midwest, there are probably more nonunion jobs available than union ones. So if you're looking for your kid to have a high volume of auditions and easy access to work, you're more likely to find that by staying nonunion. However, in this world the jobs won't pay quite as much as their union counterparts, so there's less financial reward. You and your child might put in the same amount of time and effort into professional acting, but earn less than if they were booking union work. Just something to consider.

Another thing about pay rates is that nonunion producers tend to pay children less than adults. There is no scale, or minimum rate, in the nonunion world, and producers offer whatever they think actors will accept. Sometimes the rates are very low, and often macroeconomic circumstances are used to justify lowball rates. Union producers must pay scale, so there's more predictability if you're union.

But that's only a benefit if your child is booking a lot of union work. There are many of stories of actors who go union too soon. They're perfect for one particular job, but are not ready to expand beyond whatever helped them book it. This can be discouraging and lead to burnout. Kids are not immune to this.

Honestly though, the decision of whether or not to go union is pretty black and white when it comes to doing television. All the scripted shows that shoot here are union! If your child books one of them as their first union gig, that will make them Taft-Hartley'd. If they get really lucky and are asked back in future episodes, they'll eventually have to become a member. The good news is that you'll have the money to pay for it!

Wrap Up

Everything I've written thus far has been for actors who follow the typical path in Chicago, meaning nonunion to union. In case you're wondering, there are actors who go the other way. They join the union and find that they're not booking the amount of work they thought they would for a variety of reasons. If an actor wants to step away from their membership, the union has a process for that. You can find out how by contacting the union office.

CHAPTER 15

An Actor's Income

If you've jumped to this chapter without reading any of the previous ones, I don't blame you. We're talking about getting your kid into a business where they're paid good money for having fun! But if you skipped ahead, do yourself a favor and at least read the chapter on unions. Understanding pay rates will be a lot easier if you have some details about SAG-AFTRA.

Like everything else in this business, there's a ton of variation in the amount of money that any one actor can make. Many, many factors determine an actor's income level: whether an actor is union or nonunion, what kind of work the actor books, what "type" the actor is, how old the actor is, how well the nation's economy is doing, which agent (or agents) the actor is with, how long the actor has been in the business, how well-trained the actor is, and on and on.

We all know that there's a lot of uncertainty in this business. What's interesting is that this applies to famous actors as well as the rank-and-file. It's hard to talk about averages, since even accomplished talent can experience dramatic swings in income from year to year. Sharon Wottrich, former owner of a voiceover talent agency, tells stories about voice talent whose annual incomes rocketed to

$750,000 virtually overnight and then crashed down to $250,000. These are extreme examples, but they illustrate the unpredictability of acting for a living. And if you're thinking, "I'd be pretty happy if I made $250,000," I'm thinking that, too. But if your family lived a $750,000 lifestyle, a mere quarter million would seem pretty low. It's all relative.

I can't tell you how much the average Midwest-based actor makes in a year, though I'm sure it isn't north of two hundred grand. Although there are actors who can earn a million dollars in a year, there are also those who are lucky to make a thousand.

Specifics

A lot of money is made in the Midwest acting market. Literally every day, there are multiple productions in the works and all of them are paying actors for their participation. Many of those actors are kids, and they're paid well for their time and effort.

You've learned that there are a few different categories of work in which actors can participate besides working in theatre. As we talk about exactly how much your child can make in each of them, keep in mind your own situation. Are you making major sacrifices to allow this acting thing to happen? If so, it'll help to know where the greatest potential is to get back some of what you're putting in. You also might find it helpful to know what kinds of work pay less so you can make an informed decision about whether to take those auditions when they come up. There's no rule that says your child has to do everything! You get to pick and choose.

Commercials

Actors all across the country count on commercials for at least a portion of their income. Union actors depend on the residuals to smooth out a bumpy income stream. Nonunion actors cite them as a reason they can avoid supplementing their acting work with other jobs. The earning potential is higher for union talent, but nonunion actors can still make a pretty good buck for a day's work.

A note about the following information: Every three years new rates are negotiated for each union contract. I'll use the current rates for our examples, but if you need the most up-to-date ones, check the union's website.

Union Commercials

SAG-AFTRA members can count on a nice chunk of change when they appear in a commercial, even if they're just paid scale. Currently a fee of $783.10 is paid per shoot day, per spot. This is called a session fee.

But under the union's rules, actors are also compensated for the ongoing use of their likeness and voice. These residual payments are calculated based on where and on what platform the commercial runs. As much as I'd like to say that determining earnings from union commercials is easy, it's not. This is because of the how union's commercials contract is set up.

Picture a simple ice cream sundae. You've got vanilla ice cream, hot fudge and maybe some whipped cream and a cherry on top. It's the perfect size, just big enough to do the job on a hot summer night. Everyone loves a sundae!

AIC FOR KIDS AND PARENTS — Chris Agos

For decades, the union's commercial contract was like that. Simple and easy to understand, it was initially written in the early days of television to cover actors doing live commercials during variety shows. But over time, as media matured and commercials started showing up in more places, new provisions made things a lot more complicated. That simple sundae became a gutbuster. The single scoop was joined by twenty different flavors, and all kinds of candy, salty snacks, syrups, cookies and brownies were mixed in or poured on top. Worse, with all these "improvements" came unwelcome complexity and cost increases. In the end, very few people ordered this sundae anymore.

By 2022 the industry and the union recognized the need to make some changes. They did so by leaving part of the legacy contract in place, but creating a new payment structure. This was done not only to simplify things but also to keep up with the new realities of the advertising landscape, and to open new projects to union actors.

Important Terminology

Calculating residual payments can be tricky because of the number of variables involved. It'll help if you understand a few key concepts. I'm going to give you a brief overview of the most important ones, and then we'll go through a real-world example of how an actor's residuals are paid.

Platforms

For years, advertisers have been moving away from traditional TV

An Actor's Income

networks like NBC, ABC, CBS, and FOX. These are considered the broadcast networks, meaning their signals travel over the air and not digitally through a wire. The industry uses the term "broadcast" to describe them, so we will, too.

Even though their role in an actor's pay is severely diminished compared to years past, the broadcast networks are still a large part of the advertising landscape. They are important enough that they have their own pay structure for residuals, called Class A. An example of this type of use occurs when a commercial airs from a network's national feed and goes to every network affiliate at the same time. These happen during live sports events, morning shows, news broadcasts and the like.

In the past, most ad dollars went to these networks, but now advertisers spend much more on digital media. As a result, the union has categorized the different types of available digital media, and come up with a set of rates for each of them. The types are: traditional digital, streaming, and gaming, AR/virtual worlds, and emerging platforms.

Traditional digital platforms include social media and places we used to think of as websites. Think Facebook, Twitter, even YouTube, although the premium version of YouTube is classified as a streamer. Streaming platforms are those that stream content similar to the traditional broadcast networks, but over an Internet connection. These are services like Hulu, Apple TV+ and Tubi.

The union has grouped some other digital platforms into a third category called gaming, AR/virtual worlds, and emerging platforms. These include platforms like the Sony Playstation,

Meta's Oculus, and new platforms and devices which haven't yet been invented.

The cable networks represent a different platform. They're commonly sold as part of a package of channels and are delivered to your home either via satellite or with a literal cable that runs from the street to your house. These are networks like CNN, HGTV, and Discovery. Some of these cross over into the streaming category with examples like Discovery+ and NatGeo, which is part of Disney+.

Sides Of The Contract

There are two sides to the commercials contract, the linear and linear plus digital. There are a set of provisions that just apply to commercials made for linear networks (broadcast and cable) but honestly no one makes commercials just for these outlets anymore. Nearly all commercials are produced for the linear plus digital side of the contract, so that's what we're going to talk about from here on out.

Cycles

Advertisers buy the right to use a commercial in cycles, or blocks of time. The contract allows for an advertiser to buy cycles that last 4 weeks, 13 weeks, or 1 year. This is true across most media types, and there are separate rates for each type. This means that if a client wants to buy time on network, cable and traditional digital, they can do that by paying three different rates, but they all are likely to be on the same cycle. A cycle usually begins the first day a commercial is used.

The Maximum Period Of Use (MPU)

When a company hires your kid to be in their commercial, there's a time limit placed on their use of your kid's likeness and voice. It's called the maximum period of use, and it is 21 months. It begins either the first day the commercial is used, or 13 weeks after the last day of the commercial's production.

During the MPU, your child may get holding fees. These "hold" them for a product category and enforce a product conflict, meaning they can't appear in commercials for competing brands. The session fee is considered the first holding fee, but additional holding fees are due every 13 weeks during the MPU if the commercial is not airing anywhere. If it is being used, then your child's holding fee may not be due until 1 year after the last day of your shoot, or the 1-year anniversary of the first day the commercial was used, whichever is earlier. Holding fees are typically applied as credits to residual payments. More on that later.

Holding fees are paid on commercials produced for all media types except for traditional digital platforms and gaming, AR/virtual worlds, and emerging platforms. As such, there can be no exclusivity for commercials that only run on these platforms. If there's no conflict in place, your child can work for the brand's competitors while their commercial is running.

AIC FOR KIDS AND PARENTS — Chris Agos

Edits

Trickier than figuring out compensation is determining what qualifies a commercial to be different from a previous one, so we can know when to expect to be paid for multiple spots instead of just one. For example, say your child is booked for one spot, and in it they are riding a tricycle in a scene. On the day, two versions are shot. In the first, the trike is red and in the second, it's blue. But while shooting both of them, your kid does the same action and says the same lines. The only thing that changed was the color of the trike. Does that mean two commercials were made instead of one?

The union has gotten very specific about changes like this, because it can make the difference between an actor being paid for one spot, or for more. Honestly this is getting into the weeds so if you're curious about what makes one spot different than another, visit the SAG-AFTRA site to get the details. As the parent of the actor, it's your responsibility to bring it up to your child's agent if you suspect multiple commercials might have been made.

An Example

Congratulations! Your child has been hired to do one TV spot for Target, a large national retailer. They're based in Minneapolis, so they fly you and your kid to the frozen tundra (or maybe it's nice out because it's summer) for the shoot. Your young actor will be paid a session fee for the travel day, and let's assume the shoot took one day of work and they flew you home that night. That means the total for the session is $783.10 times two, or $1566.20. Unfortunately, parents don't get paid.

An Actor's Income

Target wants to get some Class A use, so they buy a package of placements from the networks. Class A is paid by the use. The session fee includes the first use, but after that, we're paid on a sliding scale.

Class A Rates

1st Use: $783.10

2nd Use: $183.19

3rd Use: $145.33

4th-13th Each use: $145.33

13-Use guarantee: $2242.42

14th-18th Each use: $137.37

Each time the spot runs, actors are paid a certain amount for that particular airing, and the cost decreases the more the spot runs. There's an option for the advertiser to buy a package of 13 uses, representing one airing per week of a 13-week cycle, so let's assume Target picks this option. That means your young performer will earn $2242.42. There is a cap on Class A payments of $20,000 in any 13-week cycle.

New for the 2022 contract is the union's flat-rate compensation system. We used to calculate our residuals by determining where the spot runs and how many eyeballs could potentially see it. But now, we're paid a flat rate for just about anything except Class A. For the rest of our example, we'll be using flat rates to figure out how much your child will earn.

AIC for KIDS and PARENTS — Chris Agos

In a 13-week cycle, Target certainly wants to get the ad out there more than 13 times. Doing that gets expensive with Class A so there's another way clients will air the spot, and it's called the wildspot buy. With a wildspot, Target can run the spot an unlimited number of times in specific cities, but doesn't control the time of day they air. For a 13-week wildspot buy, actors earn $2000 in residuals.

Next they want to hit some cable channels and since they're a national retailer, Target is likely to buy time at the national level. There are options to buy local cable, too, but that's for smaller advertisers. Target wants the full boat, so they'll pay $4100 for 13 weeks of unlimited airing on national cable.

Now let's talk about digital platforms and streaming. Remember that there are three different media types, but only two sets of flat fees for them. This is because use in the third category (gaming, AR/virtual worlds, and emerging platforms) is included when an advertiser pays for use on streaming platforms.

Target wants to place their ad everywhere. So they pay $1100 for traditional digital use, and $2550 for streaming use.

Let's put it all together. The session payment came to $1566.20. The total for the all the uses on a 13-week cycle is $11992.42. Remember, though, that one day's worth of your session fee acts as a holding fee and is therefore credited toward residuals. Holding fees can be applied to any media type, but only once per cycle. To account for this, we'll subtract $783.10 out of that total above, leaving your young actor with $11209.32. Add the full session fee to that number and this Target job is worth $12775.52 Not bad for a couple days' work!

An Actor's Income

Remember that this is for a 13-week cycle, so if Target wants to keep the spot running beyond that, they'll have to start the process over for the next cycle, which could be another 13 weeks, or it could be 4 weeks or 1 year. If the company doesn't air the spot but still wants the *option* to air it, they'll owe a holding fee every 13 weeks until they air it again, they release the spot (retire it forever), or until the MPU expires.

This example is useful for you to see how the higher end of the union commercial spectrum works, but there are a lot of spots made that won't get that kind of airplay. I don't want you to come away thinking that every TV spot will make your child over 12 grand every 13 weeks for years. Spots that run locally and regionally don't make that kind of money. I've made plenty of commercials that paid a session and just a few hundred dollars worth of use. But I've also had spots earn a lot more than our example. It just depends on what kind of work you book. If an actor booked one job that pays $25,000 in a year, I would think of that as a jackpot.

Hold Off On The Shopping Spree

There's no guarantee that your child's spot will ever air. There are cases where the actor is paid for the session but receives no residuals. Many commercials are made but never see the light of day. They are shot and edited together, but are shelved before they air. Sometimes this is because they don't test well with focus groups.

Actors can also be edited out of commercials. When this happens, it's called a downgrade, and it means that for whatever reason, an actor is not seen or heard in the final edit. This can happen for a variety of reasons, but often occurs in spots where many actors were hired as principals. Think street scenes, crowd scenes, and party scenes. The only bright side to this situation is that actors get a downgrade fee equal to one session fee, but then the money stops. Thankfully this is pretty rare. When it does happen, it feels like someone kicked you in the gut. I know because it's happened to me.

But Wait, There's More!

Advertisers pay other fees in addition to the ones actors receive. In our example, Target will contribute about 20% of what they're paying your child toward their health and retirement benefits. Actors need to qualify for these benefits by working, and the Target job is valuable since it's possible to qualify from just that one booking.

Can Target run the spot forever? Technically yes, but they'll pay for the privilege. As mentioned previously, there's a time limit on how long the spot can run. The maximum period of use is there to protect performers from being bound to the advertiser for life. When it expires, they'll have to ask for your permission to renew it. Pretty cool. Even cooler is that an agent will only let an actor say "yes" if Target gives them a raise. Often it's 25%, but sometimes it's more. This means that if the spot continues to air beyond the MPU, holding fees and residuals will be at least 25% more than they were before.

Once they agree to a raise, another 21-month period begins. If they want to renew a second time, your child will get another one, and they'll continue to get holding fees and residuals until it's time

An Actor's Income

to renew a third time, and on and on. You can see that eventually this will get pretty expensive for Target, and sooner or later they'll release the spot, which is what happens when they no longer want to air it. At this point the spot's life will come to an end.

Never-ending holding fees sound great, but there are situations where they're less than ideal because of the conflict rule. A long time ago I did all the voice over work for a small regional wireless carrier. It was a nice gig for me. After about three years, which is a long time in this business, they decided to use someone else as their voice. As a farewell gift, they asked me to appear on camera in one spot. I was glad to do it, but what I didn't know was how long they were going to hold it. They held that thing way past the first 21 months ended, but they never aired it. I got holding fees, but no residuals.

That one spot took me out of the running for doing any TV (VO or on camera) for any other wireless provider. At the time, AT&T and Verizon did a lot of casting in Chicago, and I had to pass on those auditions, ones that would have led to far more money than I was making from the holding fees of this one, useless little spot. I about threw a party when it was finally released.

Sometimes you want your spots to be renewed until the cows come home. When you've done a spot for a pharmaceutical, or a professional association, or a utility company, you hope they hold it forever. When a company has few competitors who advertise, that's good for actors in their spots. If there's not much advertising being done by businesses like theirs, you do the happy dance because you're getting paid *and* you probably won't have to skip auditions from similar advertisers.

The other side of that coin includes companies that advertise everywhere, all the time. These are brands like like automakers, beer brewers, insurance companies, or retailers. There's a million of each, and they all advertise. When an actor works for one, they'll be in conflict with the rest until the spot is released.

Nonunion Commercials

Typical nonunion commercials pay between $300 and $600 per spot for the session. Agents try to get buyout fees in place of residuals, but they're not always successful. If they are, the buyout could double or triple what an actor makes for the session. In exchange for the buyout, the client can air the spot everywhere as often as they want without making any additional talent payments. So if the session was $500 and the buyout $1500 for a year of use, the total earnings for that spot would be $2000. Again, not bad for a day's worth of work in front of a camera.

If an agent can't get a buyout, actors earn a session fee and nothing more. The client can air the spot as long as they want without paying anything else, ever again. Some spots air for years. In cases like these, agents will likely get in touch with the client to ask for more money, but the client is under no obligation to pay anything beyond the session fee unless the spot was negotiated to run for a limited time. There are no holding fees in the nonunion world, and no health and retirement contributions, either.

Free bargaining rules the nonunion roost. That means your child's agent can negotiate for as much as they can get for session fees, buyouts, lifts and other kinds of uses. Usually advertisers who hire nonunion talent do so because it's a cost savings, not to mention

An Actor's Income

that it doesn't come with the task of tracking where and how often a spot runs. Instead of adding a bunch of small fees together, they'll usually offer one flat fee for everything, leaving the actor to decide if it's something they'd be willing to take.

This doesn't mean that nonunion actors get ripped off. Agents do their best to get rates comparable with union rates. Not every advertiser can pay those and there are plenty of actors who are happy to accept lower compensation.

In some cases, the nonunion agent isn't the entity negotiating the actor's pay. Rates are sometimes agreed upon between clients and casting directors. So if you book a nonunion spot by auditioning at a casting director's office, it doesn't matter which agent you're with, you'll get the same deal as everyone else in town since the casting director negotiated the deal.

Union Industrials

If commercials are the gifts that keep on giving, industrials are the practical, useful gifts from your aunt Eleanor. They're not fancy, but you're glad to get them.

Because they're not broadcast, industrials don't have holding fees or other residuals associated with them. Actors are paid a session fee and nothing more, except in certain cases. More on that later.

Industrials are usually much cheaper than commercials to produce, so more companies can afford them. Also, producers tend to be incredibly picky when it comes to casting their spots. They want just the right actor for every role, and nothing short of perfection will do. In contrast, there's less emphasis placed on the talent in industrials, and more placed on the message. Even if an actor isn't perfect for the job, they're still in the running if they give a strong audition.

Finally, I've been to commercial auditions where I was competing with a hundred other actors who looked just like me. Industrials sometimes only audition four or five actors per role. All this means the numbers work much more in our favor with industrials.

In Chicago, union industrials fall under the Corporate/Educational contract. This agreement spells out different rates for different situations. According to the union, there are two categories into which all industrials fall: Category I and Category II. The distinction between the two is the intended audience. Videos that are for the company's internal use only fall under Category I. These are usually training videos or other productions that are not used to sell products, but to inform or otherwise advise the company's workforce about a certain product, policy, or issue.

Anything that's produced with the intention of showing it to clients, potential customers, or anyone who does not work for the company falls into Category II. Those rates are a little higher than Category I. This is because the actor's work could be exposed to more viewers.

Chicago has another quirk to know about. There is a waiver to the Corporate/Educational contract that applies just to the Midwest, and it says that Category II rates can only be applied in the City of Chicago and its collar counties. Category I rates are in effect for the rest of Illinois, as well as the surrounding states of Wisconsin, Iowa, and Indiana. Effectively if the shoot location is

An Actor's Income

outside of Chicago and its surrounding counties, actors will only get Category I rates. But keep in mind that everything is negotiable.

The union's contract also considers what role an actor is hired for. There are background actors, day players, and narrators. Background players are extras and don't have lines. They earn $144 for an eight-hour day whether the shoot falls into Category I or II. Day players play a role while not addressing the camera. For example, in a scene that depicts a student and teacher having a discussion, both are considered day players. Category I day player rate is $551 and Category II is $686. A narrator's job is to look directly into the camera while delivering the script and provide most of the information the video is trying to get across. Narrator scale is $1002 and $1189 per day for Categories I and II respectively.

Recently, agents have been negotiating an additional fee if the video is intended to be posted online. These fees could increase an actor's paycheck by 50% or more. If there's some additional aspect to the project, like a print shoot for online ads, there will be an extra fee for that use. The details on paying actors for work that will be distributed electronically (online or streamed on wireless devices) are still being worked out by the unions. For now, it's up to the agents to negotiate deals, and it's up to the actors to take them or not.

Lastly, most often the producer will ask actors to bring some wardrobe options to industrial shoots. Plan on bringing at least a few of whatever you're asked to bring. For your trouble you'll be paid $19 for each look that winds up on camera.

You might think that industrials can be used forever, but you'd be wrong. They have a maximum period of use just like commercials.

AIC for KIDS and PARENTS — Chris Agos

Category II projects can be used for three years, beginning 90 days after the last day of the project's production. After that they must be renewed by negotiation. Category I projects can be used in perpetuity.

Keep Your Contracts

Many, many years ago I was hired by an ad agency to appear in a few videos for a certain product line. I'd love to tell you what it is but I'm legally bound not to disclose the company, so unfortunately some of the details will be deliberately vague.

I appeared on-camera as the narrator where I talked about some products and demonstrated how to use them. The first round of these videos were pressed onto DVDs and included with the products when they were sold at retail. The company also paid for them to play in big box stores for years. You might have seen me pitching these things if you walked by a little TV sitting on an end cap, rolling our videos.

Apparently the videos were working for the company, so they hired me to do more of them. I eventually appeared in or voiced over 130 of them. Each time I went to a shoot, I signed a contract. And each time, I got a copy of those contracts, brought them home, and put them in a drawer. Very early in my career I got into the habit of keeping everything related to the jobs I did, because I was told that you never know when you might need it.

One day I got an email from a friend that read, "I was shopping online for this thing and there you were, showing me how to use it!" That sounded strange because I didn't have anything airing for

An Actor's Income

that product. At least I didn't think I did. But sure enough, the old videos had made their way onto the brand's current Amazon store and it made me wonder where else they wound up. I found them on their official YouTube channel, as well as on the brand's corporate website. And they all had been there for over a decade.

Funny, because I hadn't been paid for any of them since I shot them. I checked it out and discovered that because they were originally booked as Category II videos, each one had an MPU of 3 years. The company got the first three years with the original session fees, but the subsequent years were left unpaid.

At this point I decided to exercise my right to be compensated for the continued use of my likeness and voice. I got in touch with my agent and let them know what was coming. I dug up my original contracts and spent a lot of time taking screen shots of all the pages where the videos were displayed. I was careful to include the date of the screen shots to prove that the videos were active when I said they were. I also contacted the union to verify that I had a case. Once they looked everything over and agreed that they would back me up if I made a claim, I gathered all my evidence, presented it to my agent, and they reached out to the company.

To its credit, the company listened to our concerns, acknowledged that the videos fell through the cracks, and were likely forgotten about years ago. I agreed with that assertion, but I also maintained my position that they were bound by the contracts they signed, which were legacy AFTRA contracts in place at the time of the shoots. I was owed for years worth of use.

After some back and forth, I eventually was paid the full amount. It was a lifesaver. This was in 2020, when the entire entertainment industry shut down and my income cratered. But thanks to some good record keeping, a solid union contract and some free time to pull everything together, the Agos family made it through that year unscathed.

So always keep your child's paperwork, because you just never know when you'll need it.

Nonunion Industrials

If you're a nonunion actor, the pay rates are a little more straightforward. You can expect to make more for being a narrator than for being a day player, but that's about where the similarities to the union contract end. Producers and agents work out an actor's fee on a job by job basis.

Years ago, my first multi-day industrial paid $250.00 per day. I was hired to play a college kid who needed training on how to use his library's new electronic card catalog (remember, this was before the Internet was widely available). All my scenes were with another actor, who played the role of the nice librarian who had all the answers. I was considered a day player. If I were to get that same job today, it would probably pay around $400.00 per day. On camera narrators get somewhere around $750.00 per day for their work, maybe more if they're more experienced, maybe less if the client's budget is tight.

If a nonunion agent is told that the video will wind up online, they'll try to get actors a use fee in addition to the flat payment. They aren't always successful, but when they are, they can double or triple your total take-home pay.

An Actor's Income

Whether an actor is union or not, under certain circumstances they are entitled to extra money in addition to their daily rate. If the industrial requires them to work longer than eight hours, overtime will trigger an additional payment based on how long the actor works. This doesn't happen often for kids since producers try to get them wrapped up quickly. If you're required to travel to the location, all your expenses will be covered or reimbursed. Union actors are given a per diem to cover the cost of eating while traveling. Sometimes however, nonunion producers don't have the budget to pay overtime or travel costs. In these instances, you should be notified beforehand so you can decide whether the job is worth doing.

Occasionally a producer from a far off location comes to Chicago to cast, but doesn't want to pay for a flight to get actors to the shoot. This happened to me. Back in the day I did a narration job in Green Bay, Wisconsin, which is about five hours north of Chicago by car. At the audition I was told that I'd have to drive up there because there was no budget for a plane ticket. Not wanting to lose the job, I agreed to drive if they would pay for a hotel the night before the shoot. It was fine except that was the last time I worked in Green Bay. Just as well since I'm a Bears fan.

Today, I wouldn't have taken that job, but only because I now know that actors are not obligated to take everything that comes along. I didn't realize that when I was new. Some industry people will try to convince you otherwise, but they're only looking out for their own bottom line, not yours.

AIC FOR KIDS AND PARENTS — Chris Agos

Voice Over

Actors can be hired to do a number of different kinds of voice over work. Radio spots, TV spots and longer narration are the three most common kinds of jobs kids are likely to do in Chicago, though from time to time auditions will come up for gaming and animation projects.

Union VO

TV spots can be a great source of income for voice talent. Union scale for a TV voice over session is $588.90 per spot. You'll notice that this is less than the scale session fee for on camera work, because actors are less likely to be associated with a product (and thus less likely to become overexposed) just by the sound of their voice.

The union rates for voice over work follow the same system as on camera work, but they're about 25% less. Using our previous example, if your child voiced a spot for Target at scale, they'd get $588.90 for the session. If they aired it 13 times under the Class A network rates, they'd get $1734.94 for the 13-run guarantee. If we did the math of everything else in our Target example and put it all together, we'd earn a little over $8400 in residuals.

Crediting one holding fee per cycle also applies in VO. Also, if the spot isn't airing, Target would owe holding fees every 13 weeks until it started airing again. Doing two spots would double our earnings. Obviously, the fees can add up to quite a nice chunk of change. Check out the current rates on SAG-AFTRA's website. They're listed right next to the on camera commercial rates in the charts.

Radio spots pay a lot less than TV, but that doesn't mean that

An Actor's Income

medium isn't lucrative. They're recorded under a different contract, one for audio commercials. Anything that's recorded for playback on an audio-only medium falls under this contract and is commonly just called a radio spot, even if it's for something like Pandora or Spotify. Union scale for a radio session is $347.60 per spot.

In contrast to TV, radio residuals are paid based on where the spot runs, not on the number of times it runs. For example, if it airs only in Chicago, the producer can buy a 13-week wildspot package for $377.64. Just like in TV, the session fee includes the first airing, so our residual payment would be $30.04. If the spot was aired nationally on radio networks, the wildspot fee jumps to $1886.24. The spot can also be run regionally for $1138.24. And if the spot goes online for a year, the fee is $1390.40. Again, check the union's site for details.

There are no holding fees or conflicts in radio, but if the spot is renewed after its initial run of six months, voice talent are paid another session plus usage. Complicated, I know. That's why it's important to have a good agent to explain this stuff!

When we talk about narration in Chicago, we're usually referring to the industrial kind. Companies are always producing videos that need some kind of voice over narration, and once in a while they hire kids for that work. Narration is usually paid by the hour instead of by the job. Scale for this kind of session is $488 for the first hour and $128 for each additional half-hour. That's for Category I, which we know is a project only to be viewed by the company's employees. We get a little more if the public is going to see the video. Category II scale is $503.00 for the first hour and $132 for each additional half-hour.

Obviously, the longer the job takes, the more money you can earn. Many narration jobs will take about an hour to complete, but there's no shortage of longer jobs. I once narrated a video about paper products that took nearly three days to finish. It's not like I was intentionally screwing up so that I could earn a ton of money, there were just pages and pages of material to get through! I had no idea that paper was so complicated.

Like their on camera counterparts, there are no residuals on industrial narration jobs, but sometimes agents can negotiate additional fees if the video will be posted online.

Nonunion VO

Nonunion actors don't do too shabby, though they're less likely to get anything other than their session fee. Agents try to negotiate a buyout for TV spots but aren't always successful. Expect to earn around $300.00 to $500.00 per spot, and possibly double that for a buyout that may last a year or more.

When you're nonunion, the more spots you do for a client, usually the less they want to pay you per spot. They figure they're entitled to a discount because they're buying in bulk. It's up to you to decide if this is a good deal for you.

Before I joined the union, I was offered the chance to voice a package of fifteen TV spots for a client. They offered me $275.00 per spot, for a total of $4125.00. I took the deal and was happy to make that much for the two hours of effort the job required. But then I did the math and realized how much money the client saved by going nonunion. Between session fees and residuals, they would have easily spent five figures on me if I was a union performer. I

An Actor's Income

knew there were companies out there who only hired union talent, and who spent that kind of money all the time. After that job, I started thinking seriously about membership so that I could have the chance to make that much too. Under the union umbrella, there's no discount to producers if they hire you for multiple spots. There's also no discount for having a kid behind the mic instead of an adult.

Nonunion radio payments are super straightforward. We get our session fee and that's it. Expect that payment to be $200.00 to $400.00 per spot. Buyouts are sometimes offered, but less often than with TV. There are no cycles to worry about in the nonunion world, so the session payment will be the last check your child gets for that spot unless something else has been negotiated.

Along with radio, industrial narration jobs are one area where nonunion talent can earn as much, or sometimes more than their union counterparts. Again, agents try to negotiate a session fee and a buyout for a set amount of time, especially if the project is going online. If they're successful, your kid can earn anywhere from $200.00 to $500.00 for the session, and maybe double that for the buyout.

Print

I love print jobs. Where else can you get paid to sit in front of a camera and smile for a couple hours? Once again, variation is the order of the day. Most print jobs are paid by the hour, and many pay well, but not as well as on camera or VO jobs. Where we might be able to earn about $300.00 for an hour of work doing a radio spot, that same hour spent working a print shoot for a catalog might pay $200.00. Still, not bad.

Some print jobs pay a lot more than just an hourly rate. If the photos are going to be used for multiple media like online, in brochures and on point-of-purchase displays, additional usage fees may come into play. This is sort of like the union's residual system except it usually all comes at once instead of spread out over time.

As an example, I once did a job with five other actors for a company that makes back yard grills. I was booked for an afternoon, about four hours, and the shots were to be used for a bunch of marketing materials. The usage didn't include billboards or magazine ads, but they used them in pretty much every other media outlet for a term of two years. For that I got a flat rate of $1100.00. Pretty good for four hours worth of work.

I've known actors who have earned a lot more from print jobs. When I was new in the business, I had a meeting with an agent who was considering working with me for industrials. When I showed up to meet her, she welcomed me into the office and showed me to her desk, which was right next to another agent's desk. Turns out he ran the agency's print department.

During my chat with the industrial agent, the print agent was visited by an actress who wanted to thank him for getting her a job. She was thrilled to have it, but she didn't know exactly how much she was going to make. The agent did some math and gave her the good news: she cleared about $7000 for the job. I thought "Wow! What would I do with that kind of money?!" She must have read my mind because the first thing she said was, "Great! Now I can pay my taxes." That sort of put the brakes on the celebration, but I was

An Actor's Income

still amazed that you could earn that much just from getting your picture taken.

TV/Film

Student films, no-budget projects and films on SAG waivers (agreements that defer an actor's payment until the film gets distribution) won't pay much more than $100 per day, if it pays anything. Most of these auditions won't come through your agent since there's no chance they'll make a commission if you book it, and to be honest there aren't a lot of kid roles being written for these projects.

However, your agent will be the only way to get big-budget TV and film work. It will all be done under a SAG-AFTRA contract. The union has contracts for both TV and film, and as you can imagine, they have complicated payment structures. So complicated in fact, that for me to give you hard numbers beyond simple day rates would be impossible. I'll explain more on that in a minute.

When your child is booked as a principal actor (a speaking role) on a TV or film project, they'll be paid for the shoot day (the session) and they'll also get residuals for as long as the project is being reused.

Great jobs result in a nice stream of money for years. For work on a film, producers pay residuals if the movie is released in other places besides its original method of release. Think DVD, basic cable, online or on free or subscriber-based television. For work on a television show, we're paid when the show starts reruns on its original network or is released in other media. This is part of why actors go after film and TV work. A big movie or top tier TV show can bring in quite a bit of money as it's reused by the producer or distributor.

This Is The Life

I have a friend whose story you may want to hear. While he gave me permission to tell you about him, he preferred that I didn't use his name, so I'll call him Ben. Ben's experience may have come as an adult, but it's illustrative of how residuals can impact an actor's income, no matter their age.

About 20 years ago, Ben got his first film role. He landed in the cast of a hugely successful movie. Before that, Ben was an actor from Missouri who worked in St. Louis and Chicago. But after landing that part, he moved to Los Angeles to capitalize on the momentum the appearance brought him. The move was a smart one. Over the years Ben worked on projects as diverse as sitcoms, hour-long dramas, movies of the week and big budget films.

Ben's done a lot of work, but he's not famous. If you saw him on the street you probably wouldn't recognize him, and you definitely wouldn't know his name if you heard it. But he makes a darn good living. In one recent year, Ben earned $170,000. During that year he worked about 36 days. Six weeks! The rest of the time he was off. Residuals make these kinds of numbers possible.

Ben's six weeks' worth of work made him about $35,000 in session fees. The rest of the money came from residuals from his past jobs. He made about $135,000 in residual income from TV and film appearances done years ago! The unions know that residuals can be critical to an actor's ability to earn a living and because

An Actor's Income

of this, they've put an elaborate system in place to make sure that whenever an actor's face is being seen, the actor is getting paid for it.

An Exception To The Rule

This doesn't apply to background performers. Only principal actors whose performance ends up in the final version of the project are entitled to residuals. Even if your child spent three weeks on a film set shooting multiple scenes, if their role gets edited out, they won't receive residuals. Unfortunately, it happens. Don't worry, they'll still be paid for the time they spent working on the production.

The Numbers

The complexity of the residual system in place for TV and film will make it impossible to get specific with numbers, but I'll do my best to explain this elaborate and confusing system. Because I'm going to keep things simple, you might find yourself wanting more information. The SAG-AFTRA website and YouTube channel will be helpful if you need to know more.

There are actually two different formulas for calculating residuals of actors appearing in TV shows and movies. They're both based on an actor's initial compensation for the project. In other words, the more we're paid at the time of the job, the higher our residuals will be.

Our compensation has a lot to do with the size of the role we'll play. In television, lowest on the pay scale are co-stars. This is because they help move the story along but are not central to the plot like a guest star would be, which is the next level up. Guest stars might even appear in several episodes. At the top of the pay scale are the series regulars, the ones who appear in every episode of a show. Film roles are a little less clearly defined and are generally just broken down into leads and supporting players.

The Formulas

Residuals can either be calculated using a fixed formula or one based on gross receipts of the project, meaning the amount the producers receive for the sale of that project to a network, streaming service, or distributor.

Most network TV shows, like NBC's *Chicago PD*, follow the fixed residual formula, which simply means that every time your child's episode airs, they'll be paid for that airing. Let's say they book a co-star role that appears in one episode. The breakdown that comes with the audition will tell you what kind of role they're auditioning for, but there are some things that can clue you into the fact that it's a co-star. If the role only has a few lines, shows up only in one scene, and doesn't have a character name in the script (it's just listed as "preschooler"), it's a co-star.

Co-stars are usually hired by the day because often their scene can be shot and wrapped in less than eight hours. For that reason they're sometimes called day players. They get a minimum of $1082 for one day of work in an hour-long show. That is the scale rate and it applies if the actor has never been hired in TV before. Once your child has a job or two under their belt, the agent can sometimes negotiate a higher rate, which is called a "quote". Your agent will not always be successful at getting this upgraded rate.

An Actor's Income

Whether your child is booked at scale or at their quote, the session payment includes the episode's first run. Residual payments are triggered when the episode runs after that. The first time the episode reruns in its regular time slot (the second actual airing), your kid is due a payment equal to half of a session fee, or $546.50. Beyond that, calculating residuals starts to get tricky. They're based on formulas that consider such variables as the contract in place at the time of the shoot, the production length and type and the market where the show appears.

Chicago PD has been sold into syndication, which means it's been bought by other networks to be aired in non-primetime slots. The formula used to figure a residual for the episode takes into account the number of times an actor has already been paid. We earn 40% of the scale day rate for the first rerun, 30% for the second, 25% for the third, and on and on until the 12th rerun. At that point we'll earn a payment of 5% of scale every time the show airs thereafter.

There are also foreign residual fees, which means the show has been sold to a free TV network based outside of the US and Canada. These residuals wind up being about 35% of a scale session fee, or about $382.50.

Remember that the value of residuals are tied to an actor's initial compensation. If your child was booked as a guest star, the residuals would be higher with that kind of role.

It's easy to see that the show in which we're cast makes all the difference. If your kid books a role on a series that's really popular, they'll make more in residual payments from that appearance because it's more likely to be rebroadcast more often. Conversely, if they worked on a show that never made it through its first season, there's not going to be much meat on that residual bone, though they still might get something. I have done several shows that were canceled after their first season, and I still get small residual checks because they continue to be broadcast on some network, somewhere in the world.

Residuals are generally paid quarterly, though in my experience there can be variations in the length of time between payments. Eventually it all works out and the union even operates a fund for residual payments that are somehow lost in the system.

Another Example

Let's take a look at the other way of calculating residuals, which is the revenue sharing method. Most high budget shows on streaming platforms like Netflix will calculate residual payments using something called the distributor's gross receipts, which is the amount producers make by selling the show to a streaming service. This number varies from show to show, but the episode's cast will share about 3.6% of this amount. The variation means these residuals are harder to calculate and ultimately predict.

Let's assume your kid books a co-star on an episode of *The Bear*. This is a 30-minute show that runs on Hulu, which is a streaming video on demand platform, or SVOD platform.

According to the contract that governs cast payments for SVOD platforms, we start by figuring our total actual compensation for the job. If we were hired at scale for one day, we may have actually earned more than just our scale session fee. At the very least the agent probably negotiated their commission into our deal, which adds 10% to our check. And if we're lucky enough to get our quote, maybe we worked for a few hundred dollars over scale. The total session fee includes that additional money, and that number is used as the basis for our residual calculation, up to a ceiling. If our compensation for an episode exceeds the ceiling, our residual will be figured using that ceiling amount. This is partially to prevent celebs who get extremely high rates from eating up a lot of the residuals. Currently the cap for a 30-minute show on an SVOD platform is around $2700 and around $4450 for an hour-long show.

In addition to covering the time we spend on set, the session fee includes the first 90 days of the episode's exhibition. After that, a clock of sorts starts ticking. The show has to pay residuals as long as it is available for audiences to view. Here's where it gets tricky.

Every streaming platform you can think of requires subscribers to operate. They report how many subscribers they have to the union in July of every year. That number is then used to calculate what's called the subscriber factor, which is expressed as a percentage. The more domestic subscribers a platform has, the higher the factor. There's a 40% tier, a 65% tier, up to a 150% tier. This accounts for the fact that not all platforms have the same number of subscribers, or eyeballs that might watch the show. Hulu's subscriber factor is 150%. So you'd take your overall initial compensation, multiply it by 150% and then take that number and multiply it again by something called your year percentage.

The year percentage refers to how long it's been since the episode was first made available on Hulu. The percentages decrease by about 5% every year, so the longer the show airs, the less money we'll make. Let's assume it's been one year since your child shot the show.

Our first year percentage is 45%. This amount declines every year until it gets down to 1.5% in year 13, after which is stays there forever. Scale for working one day on an episode of a show is currently $1082. Scale plus a 10% agent fee comes to $1190.20. Let's assume your child's booking was straightforward, and no additional fees were triggered (like overtime, meal penalties, or anything else). They were paid scale plus ten percent, so that's our starting point for the residual calculation. The math looks like this:

Overall Initial Compensation x Subscriber Factor =

$1190.20 x 150%=

$1785.30

$1785.30 x Year Percentage = your residual payment for the year.

$1785.30 x 45%= $892.65

Large platforms also pay foreign residuals. Those are paid over and above our domestic residual and work out to be about 35% of that number.

Residuals that follow this formula are paid annually, which means you can expect to get one check that covers a year's worth of use.

Film

When a large-budget film comes into town and casts local actors, they're hiring them under SAG-AFTRA's Theatrical Agreement. This contract pays actors like TV shows and commercials do in the

An Actor's Income

sense that actors get session and residual fees. Current scale for one day of work is $1082 and $3756 for a week.

Residual payments for film follow the revenue sharing method, where the entire cast splits some of the gross receipts when the film gets distribution to various media outlets, but that's only when there's enough money to share with the cast. Some films don't make enough to trigger a revenue split.

When the residual kicks in, the calculations are even more complicated than they are for TV because they give weight to actors who were paid more during production. Because of this, I won't be able to give you hard numbers, so I'll just give you the formula instead.

Film residuals are usually figured using the production's gross revenues after certain deductions are taken. That number is called the "adjusted gross". When there's enough revenue left over to share with the cast, the union uses a "time and salary" system, which is expressed in units, to figure out how to divide a portion of those revenues between cast members. The more time an actor spends on set and the more they earned for that time, the greater their share of the revenue split. The bigger the cast, the smaller the share. Big casts means more actors to share the revenue, lowering each actor's individual take.

Currently, principal actors share 3.6% of the adjusted gross when the film airs on television or is moved over to a streaming platform after initial release. If the movie is released on DVD, the residual is 4.5% of the first million dollars of the adjusted gross and 5.4% on the rest. Remember, principal actors share this number, not background players. Just to give you an example, I have friends who have worked on some of the big movies that have come through

Chicago over the years, and they report their residuals are in the low hundreds of dollars per quarter. Some report receiving less than $50 every quarter.

But not all films are shot under this particular agreement. SAG-AFTRA has contracts for producers of independent films with much lower rates than the basic agreement. Depending on the budget, an actor could get as little as $100 per day under the ultra-low budget agreement. This agreement allows for residual payments for things like Internet use, but the payments are very low. You can check out the details of this and other low budget contracts at www.sagindie.org.

The Gift That Keeps On Giving

All residual payments, no matter their calculation method, keep coming for as long as the production is generating money for the producer and the revenue generated is enough to be shared among the cast. Even after actors pass away, their heirs continue to get payments. Only when the production is mothballed and never used again will the checks stop coming. So you can see that the longer your child is working in film and TV, the more money they'll make. There are actors who still get checks from things they worked on in the 1970's!

A Word About Taxes

When kids work, they have to file their taxes at the end of the year. It's worth noting that an actor's union status will make a difference at income tax time. Nonunion work will pay in full without any withholding. That means the Internal Revenue Service will expect the actor to pay those taxes. Union jobs, on the other hand, will nearly always withhold federal, state, and local (if applicable) income taxes. The amount of the withholding will vary, but depends on a multitude of factors such as the information provided on the IRS form W-4, and the state where the job was located.

The location of the job is determined by where your child's feet are planted when they do the job. For example, a union on camera job that shoots in Chicago will have federal and state taxes withheld for Illinois. But if they're standing in St. Louis while they shoot, that triggers withholding for federal income tax, Missouri income tax, and local St. Louis income tax. That means you'll have to file taxes in Missouri as well as Illinois. If they do a VO job from your home studio in Chicago, while connecting to the client's studio in Iowa, you'll count that as a job done in Illinois, even if the payment is coming from out of state.

Make sure to ask an accountant how to handle each situation when you file at the end of the tax year.

CHAPTER 16

Advocating For Your Child

The entertainment industry is full of wonderful people. They care deeply about their families, the welfare of the production community, about doing good work and supporting everyone so that we all have a chance to advance.

But many of them are not parents. Some of them are, but when they're working, they aren't thinking like parents. In pre-production, and especially on the set, they're thinking like a director, or a producer, or a production assistant. Their jobs depend on delivering the best result for their client.

Because of this, sometimes decisions are made without considering the impact on the project's young talent. This happens to actors of all ages. It's not unusual for us to make small personal sacrifices to get the shot, or tell the story the way a client expects it to be told. Usually the discomfort involves something minor like working in temperatures that are too hot or cold given our wardrobe, but it can go a little further than that.

I briefly mentioned this before, but I was once put on a roller coaster for a shot even though I told the director that it would make me sick. He was determined to get the look and feel for the commercial that he sold to the client, and he wasn't going to let an actor's low threshold for motion sickness get in the way. I could have refused, but I went ahead with it knowing there was a chance I'd make it through the ride just fine. Sadly, the coaster was a monster and they made me do it six times. In the end I raced to the nearest trash can. The director felt bad, but we got the shot. Things like that can be part of the job, and we know that going in.

Children, though, can only be asked to go so far out of their comfort zones. As parents, it's our job to advocate for our kids. No one else will do this for us. We shouldn't expect a director, child wrangler, or set teacher to say something if it looks like a decision is being made that could jeopardize the production in some way, or expose our kids to negative experiences.

Being an advocate for your child actor can take many forms. It starts with doing what you can to make them available to work. A child can't be cast if they're not available, so scheduling flexibility is the key to making it work for everyone.

At auditions, parents should ask questions if they see a potential issue for their kid. For example, if the scene involves eating birthday cake and your child has a nut allergy, informing the casting people at the audition can help prevent any mishaps if your kid books the job. And of course, if the child is cast, it'll be critical to let the production staff know of the allergy before the shoot day.

Once on the set, protecting kids goes beyond just making sure they're safe. Monitoring who has contact with the child, what they're being asked to do, and where they're allowed to wander is important not just to protect them, but also to protect the project. We never want our kids to be the reason a shoot is thrown off track.

One Family's Outlook

Alexandra Anaya Green is an actor and mom of two young performers, ages 5 and 10. Together with her husband, Joshua, they pursue the business as a family. All four of them are frequently booked together. "Sometimes it's just the two kids and myself, sometimes it's Joshua and one of the kids, it just really depends on the job, but I make an effort to market us as a family. We can provide a one-stop talent solution for clients."

Alexandra begins advocating for her kids by making sure everyone is on the same page when it comes to their kids' schooling. "Being upfront from the beginning was really important. I explain to the administration, the teachers, anyone involved with the school that these are working children, and that means they'll require a little more flexibility." Often Alexandra will get a call asking if they can be at a shoot in as little as two hours. "I've had to pick the kids up at lunch with a fresh change of clothes to drive them to an afternoon job."

The key to avoiding the school's ire in situations like this is to make sure the children are accomplished students. "When they see that our kids are doing well enough to be on the honor roll, they're more apt to accommodate them occasionally missing school."

Being Hyper Aware

The vast majority of productions will put child safety at the top of their list of concerns. But as parents, our top priority should be to have *our child's* safety at the top of our list. Alexandra says "I am not just aware of what's going on with my kids on set, I am hyper-aware.

AIC for KIDS and PARENTS — Chris Agos

No one is going to protect my kids like I will, and it doesn't matter if I'm there as their Mom or if I'm also acting. My highest responsibility is to make sure that my kids are safe, set up for success, and taken care of. Sometimes that means speaking up."

Although stylists are often there to help change the kids into wardrobe, Alexandra handles that job to ensure hair, makeup and wardrobe are not compromised. When her young actors need to have a microphone fished through their clothing, Alexandra empowers the child to ask if they can mic themselves or she offers to do it. It's not that she doesn't trust the on-set professionals, it's that she wants to remove any risk associated with sensitive situations. "I suggest things in a nice way, from the perspective of helping instead of protecting, but in fact I'm making sure I'm always present for my kids. That's my job as their Mom."

Alexandra's sense of advocacy means she also thinks about the production and never wants to put her children in the position of possibly bringing work to a halt. "On one commercial, my youngest was asked to carry the fragile product from one place to another on the set. It was at the end of a long day and the food stylist had gone through all their hero product. These were the last ones left. If they were dropped and wound up on the floor, the shoot was over. My son was being asked to do something that was outside of his ability to execute safely." She suggested there might be another way to get the shot they were looking for without jeopardizing the client's product. The director agreed and made an adjustment to the shot.

She also tries to plan for life's little biological emergencies. "I'm trying to actively anticipate when my youngest needs to use the bathroom, because often there's only one outfit for him to wear on set. It's not like they buy multiples. If he needs to step away from set where bathrooms may not be easily accessed or has an accident, the whole production grinds to a halt as everyone waits."

The craft service table on a set can be a risky place to let kids wander on their own. It's there for the actors and crew to be able to grab something small to eat during longer shoots. It's filled with snacks of all kinds, from sweet to salty, and is often stocked with tempting drinks like sodas and juices. Alexandra is very mindful of what and how much her kids are consuming on set. "I don't allow my kids near craft services alone, or let a crew member take them over to the table. I monitor their choices because if someone chooses a food or drink that stains their hands, mouth, or wardrobe, it can compromise and delay the shoot. It's also to no one's benefit if they get a sugar rush at the wrong time."

This kind of foresight only comes with lots of experience. The Green family is busy. They sometimes do two or three auditions a day. They've traveled to three different states in the same week for work. Is this normal? Can you expect your young performers to be that involved in the business? Maybe! Some families aren't as busy as the Greens, but others are right up there with them.

Professionalism

Another way we protect kids on set is to show them what it means to be professional. We always want our kids to have fun (why else work in this business?), but they also need to know when it's time to dial up their focus to help get the job done.

AIC FOR KIDS AND PARENTS — Chris Agos

Acting is creative and collaborative, but at the core it is a service business. The people doing the hiring want what anyone does when they hire someone. They want a good experience.

If you pay someone to paint your kitchen, you expect it to look good in the end. But how the painter gets there matters just as much as the final result. If they show up late every day, eat your food, break your dishes and leave without cleaning up, it won't matter how amazing the paint job is, you're never hiring them again. Same thing with actors. Your kid can be brilliant on screen but if their off-screen antics make the day more stressful and longer than it has to be, they're not going to be invited back. Repeat business is the lifeblood of any actor's career.

Some kids are just too little to understand what being professional means. With very young children, the parent is responsible for projecting professionalism to the crew and in the process, model it for their child.

I once worked with an actor whose professional mantra was, "Be prepared, be on time, and bring a book." I think that's a great starting point for understanding what's expected of parents and their young performers.

Being prepared looks different depending on the age of the child actor and the type of job they're doing. Obviously we can't get very young kids ready for a job, but as they get older we can prepare them by explaining what's expected of them. That starts with the script, which is likely to be pretty similar to the audition. We want them to know what they're supposed to say, when they're supposed to say it, and what's happening before, during, and after they're speaking or doing their action. We just want them to know what's coming so there are no surprises.

One thing that clients love is having choices in terms of an actor's performance. No director wants to see the same performance from an actor take after take, they like a little variety. That's one of the reasons we're asked to perform our action multiple times on set. We do this in collaboration with the director, who knows what the client is looking for better than we do. So prep kids to be ready to do the script many times, and ask them ahead of time to think about a few different ways to approach it. A kid who's been in an acting class or two should be familiar with this concept.

Being on time is a no-brainer. Do you know who's allowed to be late to jobs? Clients, and that happens frequently. But actors are expected to be on time, all the time. This goes back to the idea that we never want to be the cause for on-the-job hiccups.

Another great thing parents can do for their kids is have something to occupy them on the set, because there is always a lot of waiting. Idle time can lead to boredom, which is never a good thing. Having books, games, and other activities at the ready can help keep kids from wandering, being noisy, or getting too silly because there's nothing for them to do while the rest of the cast and crew work the set.

Stacey Apfel, Mom to sisters Alivia and Elly Goldberg, says "I always pack their favorite snacks and make sure to bring their iPads with headphones, so we don't disturb others on set. When the girls were younger they played games to stay occupied, now it's more streaming. I also make sure they bring their homework so they don't fall behind."

AIC for KIDS AND PARENTS — Chris Agos

It's a good idea to bring along any necessities, like a change of clothes, extra diapers (if needed), and any medication the child might require. If your child is allergic to animals but will be working with one on set, make sure to bring whatever they need to get them through that situation. I have a friend whose daughter is very allergic to bee stings, so their EpiPen is always with them, even if the shoot is inside on a sound stage.

The truth is that even the most well-behaved kids sometimes fall off the good behavior wagon for various reasons. To a certain extent, very young actors are given a pass for bad or distracting behavior because, well, they're kids! But if things get too distracting, everyone relies on the parent or guardian to handle the situation and bring the kid back down to Earth.

Unfortunately that's not always possible. I once did a print job where I played the father of two, a bright eight-year-old girl and a super cute boy of about three. These kids were siblings in real life, and they were accompanied to the job by their Mom.

The shoot started well enough, but at one point the little boy started getting antsy. He was just being a normal, unpredictable little kid. The Mom tried a few things to refocus him, from snacks to breaks to bribes, but nothing worked. This went on long enough that the atmosphere started getting tense. Multiple adults tried to address the situation, but the little guy wasn't having any of it. Even the sister tried consoling him, which seemed to buy us a little more time.

Eventually the photographer needed a shot of me sitting in an easy chair, reading to the kids. He wanted the girl standing next to the chair and the boy in my lap, quietly listening. The kid was bouncing around the set like it was a playground, but the team decided to push forward and shoot around his energy bursts. I sat down, the girl took her place, and their Mom plopped the boy down onto my lap. And then he looked up at me and punched me in the nose, hard enough to make it bleed.

One thing a professional actor does is protect the wardrobe. I put my hand up to prevent anything from staining my sweater, which they had bought for me to wear that day. The stylist rushed over with tissues to stop the nosebleed. There were lots of apologies but at this point the Mom didn't seem to know what to do and practically gave up trying to control her son. She literally threw her hands up in the air as he ran to the door, opened it, and left the building.

He didn't get far and when everyone came back, he was a little calmer. His hands were dirty and he had dusty stains on the knees of his pants. The stylist cleaned him up and we tried again. This time he swatted at me and scratched my ear with his little fingernails.

At this point in my career I wasn't a Dad, but I knew a lost cause when I saw one. I walked over to the photographer and quietly said, "Does everyone need to be in the shot?" There was a conference between the clients and the Mom and it was decided I would read the book to his sister instead.

When things like this happen, it reflects badly on the parent even though everyone knows that kids will be kids. That may not sound fair, but there's a responsibility that comes with declaring to the world that you and your kid deserve to be paid for doing a job. Everyone is allowed to have a bad day, but it's expected that parents have some influence over their kids. And if a child lashes out at

AIC FOR KIDS AND PARENTS — Chris Agos

others when they're unhappy, that's a tendency parents likely know about before they accept a job. It was irresponsible to put that little boy in that situation at that time.

According to one producer I spoke with, disruptive performers and ineffective parents are remembered. "We have a list," he said. "On it are names of families we just can't work with again. There's too much at stake both economically and relationship-wise with our clients to give people second chances."

Of course, part of being professional means parents need to help their kids focus (and refocus) without adding to the on-set frustration. In our example, the Mom at least had the wherewithal to keep her cool with her son. Yelling, demeaning, or otherwise getting aggressive with kids just makes the situation worse for everyone.

Alexandra Green says her husband has a trick to keep their kids focused. When he senses them heading in the wrong direction, he says, "The director really wants that energy for the job. You have to save it for when the camera's rolling! We don't want you to waste it, so keep it for when they ask you for it." Genius.

CHAPTER 17

Child Actors And Social Media

Parents of young performers often wonder whether their kids need to be active on social platforms. It is a requirement for a child actor to have lots of followers and viral posts? The answer, as you might expect, is complicated.

Those who make the case that social media is a must for kids in this business point to the benefits of exposure. No matter their age, an actor can increase their chances of getting work by increasing their visibility. Before we had social media, visibility only came with appearances in projects like TV shows, commercials, and feature films. Today, we can create our own visibility by building an audience on the platform of our choice.

There are lots of stories about casting decisions coming down to two actors, with the job ultimately going to the one with the larger social following. Producers figure that if an actor comes with a built-in audience, some of those eyeballs are going to watch the project just because that actor is involved. That may or may not be true, but it's the perception that matters.

However, having a large social following is neither required to have an active career, nor is it a guarantee of future work. High follower counts don't automatically translate into a high number of bookings. Casting decisions usually still come down to the actor who's most right for the job based on an audition.

It's The Parent's Choice

A lot of families have reservations about letting their kids participate in social media, and it's easy to understand why. On top of the research that's out there about the negative impact it can have on kids and teens, parents sometimes see changes in their children after giving them access. One Mom confided in me that, "Getting a phone changed my daughter and her view of the world in ways I didn't expect. I wish I could take it back."

The reality is that social media was created for adults, so just like the world of professional acting, having our kids active on social platforms is just another adult environment we're asking them to navigate.

Whether to open social accounts for kids is up to their parents and no one else. It is not a decision to be left up to an agent, manager, casting director, or acting teacher. People in those positions might want the best for a child's career, but they won't see the potential lasting impact social media may have on that child, if any.

Our son has a phone, but no social media. We're just not there yet, and frankly neither is he. The way we look at it is this: He's got the rest of his life to be active on social. If he misses a job or two because he's not participating now, we're fine with that. So don't feel pressured to join every social platform out there.

Diving In

If you do decide to open social accounts for your young performer, there are some best practices to follow. When my wife was growing up in small town Illinois, her Mom had a saying: "Never do anything you don't want to read about in the newspaper." Replace the newspaper with the Internet and that's still good advice today.

Before you register on any platform, parents should do a sweep of their own social accounts. Check Facebook, Instagram, and anywhere else you frequently post to make sure there isn't anything you might not want your child, their friends, or their potential industry partners (agents, clients, etc.) to see. Assume that anyone who's considering working with your child will vet the family to make sure it's safe for their show or brand. While you're at it, make sure your kid isn't tagged in any photos that you don't want visible to the general public, and wipe any personal information that might be posted, like locations, addresses, phone numbers, and school names. It's not a bad idea to do this with all the social accounts connected to the family, including any siblings and step parents. The idea is to start with a clean slate and make it as difficult as possible for a casual observer to uncover specifics that you want to keep private.

Take the extra step of registering the domain version of your child's name. You want to own yourchildsname.com if it's available. If it's taken, consider going with some other registration like .tv or

.net. You don't have to turn it into a full blown website right away, but it's nice to have the option down the road.

Finally, turn off location sharing on your phone. When you start posting, you don't want your exact location being broadcast to the world. There is never a need for the general public to know your child's location patterns.

Parent-Run Accounts

Unless your actor is a mature teen, it's best for parents to act as a buffer between the account and the outside world. We always want to have an adult overseeing the public image of a child. Besides that, the terms of use for most of the social platforms require users to be at least 13 years old.

I'm sure you're seen something like, "Account run by Mom" in social bios. This allows control over not only what comes in from other users, but also what gets posted, how long kids spend on the platform, and what other accounts the child is interacting with. We definitely want young actors to have a say in what gets posted and who gets followed, but final decisions should be left up to someone who understands the implications of what's being presented and who the account is interacting with.

Posting, Following, Engaging

As a general rule, a young actor's social accounts should be devoted their work as an actor. That doesn't mean you can only post shots of them on stage or in front of a camera, but you do want to keep the content focused. Think of it like an extended resume. The

Child Actors And Social Media

information viewers get should be current and relevant to why they're there in the first place. They probably didn't come to see your kid hit a triple in her softball game. They're there to see what she's up to performance-wise. Post the softball videos on your own profile as a proud parent.

It's a good idea to avoid posting a few other things. Auditions are a no-no. Never post anything about an audition including what it's for, which agent sent it your way, and especially not the script, which are never for public consumption. That ad agency or television writer does not want their work out there for the general public to see until it's shot, edited, and released on their timeline.

Once your child is on set, no doubt you'll have some great pictures to share. But make sure you get the permission of whoever's in the photos as well as the production manager before posting. Every show has a different policy about actors posting photos, so check to make sure it's allowed in your case. Sometimes they don't even want you to post a shot of your child in wardrobe, even if there's nothing in the picture that's going to give anything away about the project.

Also, you may be tempted to post your child's work once it's out in the public domain, but you have to be careful with this. Whoever owns the copyright on that content has control over how it can be used, meaning you need permission to post a clip from a movie or episode of a TV show. Sometimes producers will distribute clips to the cast and ask them to post it, but if that doesn't happen, don't assume you're welcome to post. Check with your agent first. And don't ever, ever post any industrial or commercial unless you are given written consent from the client. When in doubt, hold off on posting content that isn't yours.

AIC FOR KIDS AND PARENTS — Chris Agos

Give some thought to how the profile is going to be seen by the industry. You know your kid better than anyone, so who are they? Are they mischievous and loaded with attitude? Driven and always striving to do better? Super sweet and bubbly? However they show up in real life is how they should show up on social media. If there's such a thing as a social "brand", this is where we start developing one.

You'll want to follow accounts that share something in common with your young performer. Of course you'll follow the talent agencies, performance schools, and other industry connections you make over time. But you also will want to follow other young actors your child may meet in class or on jobs, as well as the adults they wind up working with, too. Following directors and casting folks isn't a bad idea, just don't do so thinking that you're increasing your kid's chances of working with them. The business doesn't work that way. No casting director calls a kid for an audition simply because they follow them on Instagram. If they see something on an account that makes it seem like a kid might be right for a role they're casting, then maybe they'll reach out. But that's usually only if they can't find what they need through traditional channels, otherwise known as talent agencies.

Whatever accounts you choose to follow, you'll want to engage with them a little. This can be liking, commenting on, and sharing the posts of others, but it is not direct-messaging people. Of course if you have a relationship with someone, feel free to message them all you want. But good etiquette says parents don't hit up casting directors or other industry insiders to recommend their kids.

Keep It In Perspective

Social media is great for making and maintaining connections, which can sometimes lead to real-world jobs. What social media shouldn't do is become your young actor's main thing. It can become a grind, so don't let it replace the work of being an actor. Being a social media star is very different from being an actor. The industry has discovered this multiple times. For a while YouTubers and social stars were being cast in scripted projects over actual actors. The results weren't always positive, which is why producers have become more careful about casting them.

Don't feel like having social accounts is a make-or-break situation for your child's acting career. I've seen parents post multiple times a day on all platforms, and it sends the wrong message. It's fine for children to have profiles, but we don't want to present them as desperate for attention. Sometimes we put a little too much emphasis on social, and the reality is that your child still has to be willing and able to do the work of an actor. Their time is probably better spent in class than creating social content.

CHAPTER 18

Wrap Up

The thing that has kept me in this business for more than 25 years is also the thing that keeps my son engaged in it. This industry is loaded with potential. It is vast, wide, and open to everyone.

Every day, thousands of projects are simultaneously being worked on all across the country. Most of them will be nearly invisible to the general public. Some will become important to a large group of people, and others might well turn into cultural touchstones. It's exciting to think that we can be a part of that.

The entertainment and advertising industries support many types of careers. Your kid might get their start working in front of a camera, but they could become a director, writer, agent, animator, sound designer, key grip, camera operator, on-set acting coach, editor, costume designer, drone pilot, music supervisor, precision driver, publicist, studio head, showrunner, or any of dozens of other available careers. As time passes, there are going to be new jobs no one's even thought of yet.

This is the kind of opportunity that I want for my kids. I want them doing something they love in an industry that values and rewards their hard work. What's the old saying? "If you love what you do, you'll never work a day in your life."

But obviously, a child's acting career doesn't have to be forever. Plenty of kids work here and there, put some money away for college, and move on to other things. There's certainly no shame in that.

And it's true that this business agrees with some folks, and others find that it's not really for them. If that winds up describing you and your family, it's so much better to learn that early on.

I hope the information in this book has been a valuable part of your discovery process. I use the word "process" because an actor's journey through this business is just that. Even after working for more than a quarter century and writing a bunch of books, I'm still discovering new things. I think that's part of the fun.

I wish you and your young performer(s) nothing but the best. May you find the success you deserve!

Acknowledgments

Many people helped write this book. Thanks to Rachel Patterson, Mary Franke, Carole Dibo, Sean Bradley, Anne Acker, and Michael McCracken for sharing their thoughts on the education of child actors. Parents Stacey Apfel, Allison Hoppe, and Alexandra Anaya Green provided critical input from their own experience raising young performers. Jenny Wilson helped clarify all things having to do with reps. Ed Kross and Richard Schoen are professionals whose career anecdotes shed light on certain topics in the book. Tracey Hunt clarified the myriad of rules surrounding the State of Illinois Minor Employment Certificate program. And finally, this book wouldn't exist without my wife Patricia's encouragement, and the experience we've gained from stewarding our sons through the industry. I can't thank them enough.

www.ingramcontent.com/pod-product-compliance
Lightning Source LLC
Chambersburg PA
CBHW070639160426
43194CB00009B/1507